SUSSEX TAI
MYSTERY AND
MURDER

SUSSEX TALES OF MYSTERY AND MURDER

W. H. Johnson

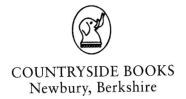

COUNTRYSIDE BOOKS
Newbury, Berkshire

COUNTRYSIDE BOOKS
3 Catherine Road
Newbury, Berkshire

To view our complete range of books,
please visit us at
www.countrysidebooks.co.uk

ISBN 1 85306 744 X

Produced through MRM Associates Ltd., Reading
Typeset by Mac Style Ltd, Scarborough, N. Yorkshire
Printed by J. W. Arrowsmith Ltd., Bristol

Contents

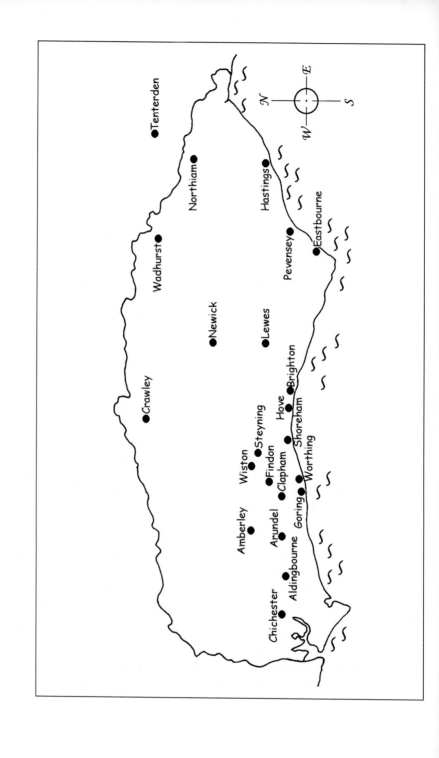

INTRODUCTION

I have had great pleasure from writing this book. Odd, you may think, for certain of the chapters demonstrate some of the worst human failings – greed, cruelty, disloyalty. But a book of this kind is not simply about excesses of wickedness for I have included too some instances of fine human behaviour.

For example, I have been impressed over the years by the resilience of Colin Wallace, the former Intelligence Officer, who after suffering years of imprisonment with dignity and spirit was ultimately cleared of all responsibility for the killing of his friend. And my researches into the murder of Inspector Walls in 1912 have introduced me to DCI Elias Bower, a canny detective whose subtle handling of two very unreliable witnesses ultimately led to a conviction.

And I have wondered with great admiration at the sheer nerve of witchcraft investigator Charles Walker, who accepted the invitation to meet one dark night in the depths of woodland a stranger who claimed to have information on black magic practices. Few of us would have ventured alone into such a menacing place, a wood in which there had been unexplained deaths and where only weeks earlier a man had disappeared.

This business of witchcraft, a mystery to most of us, crops up in the account of the curious happenings at Newick not so many years ago. Of course, there was a great degree of sharp practice here but no one can doubt that the Satanist Derry Knight told some truths about his awful allegiance to the Devil. It is a sobering thought that as we live our unremarkable everyday lives others have seriously dedicated themselves to the worship and pursuit of evil.

As for other aspects of the supernatural, I have included the intriguing tale of young Alan Rhodes, the focus of quite alarming poltergeist activity in his Crawley home. And there is the case of the disturbances in a Brighton flat which a team of spiritualists visited in order to seek an explanation and remedy matters.

What a strange affair that was out at Aldingbourne. Even though the evidence and documentation is sparse, there is enough to suggest a rattling good mystery. Spontaneous human combustion – is that what it was? And then there's the ghost at Amberley Vicarage. I was on the point of describing this as a 'charming' story but then recalled that there is within it a hideously dark element. Were there two bodies under the floorboards all those years?

I suppose that there may be a hierarchy of villains and murderers. We all carry in our heads the names of those at the peak of notoriety. Some of those who kill deliberately are of course less culpable than others. The three young people found guilty of that most appalling murder of a boy even younger than themselves, perhaps, sad and weak and deluded in their depravity. And how are we to feel about the man who slew his wife out of provocation or desperation or maybe as a consequence of a broken heart? Certainly the judge and jury felt some sympathy for him, recognising that although he might be a flawed character he had been put under excessive pressure.

But there are some genuinely wicked characters here. The world has not forgotten Patrick Mahon, that handsome yet heartless womaniser, at the love nest he had rented just outside Eastbourne. His is one of the celebrated tales of gruesome murder. And whilst I imagine that they will never be classics of the true-crime genre, two more recent murders cannot fail to chill the blood. For if a man's friend shoots him in the back, if a wife arranges her husband's murder, who then can be trusted? These people are the great offenders for in pursuit of their own ends they batter down all that decent societies build. These are the ones who commit the cruellest crimes. They kill those who trust them.

I have tried in spite of some of the subject matter not to be sensational in recording the facts. What the accounts do have, it seems to me, is a strong narrative drive. If I am right in making that assessment, then you will really be intrigued by what appears in the following pages.

W. H. Johnson

ACKNOWLEDGEMENTS

One of the inescapable facts of writing non-fiction is that one is always going to have to rely on so many other people. Often there is the need to check up on some minor fact, something that seems to be no more than a footnote but upon which the whole edifice of the account may depend. One frequently needs to depend very heavily on others for direction – people who can suggest further reading or additional sources of information. On occasion they may not know anything about the topic but they often do know a man – or a woman – who does. Then there are those who will provide the whole story or at least a significant part of it. In writing this book I have needed help from all these sources.

I would like to put on record my profound gratitude. First, I thank Philip Steff of Bath and Charles Walker of Worthing who are central figures in two chapters. Then there is Len Woodley of the Police History Society, who gave me such a powerful kick-start on the murder of Inspector Walls. Paul Williams has rummaged through his extensive murder files and has saved me much foot-slogging, rail-travelling and e-mailing.

The editor of the *Littlehampton Gazette* kindly provided me with the picture of Colin Wallace; The Eastbourne Society offered several pictures relating to the Walls case; the proprietor of the *Wealden Advertiser* magazine sent me a cutting of the curious advertisement which the Daddows placed in its pages just before the murder; Jo Bishop of Esprit was encouraging and the report that her group produced on Clapham Wood proved very helpful to me. Then I cannot fail to thank the many journalists, national as well as local, on whose column inches I have had to depend for much of the more recent material.

I must mention, too, Crawley Library, who came up with a gem of a story and of course the help of Martin Hayes, Principal Librarian (Local Studies) of West Sussex, and also the Rev Stephen Guise of Amberley. Sian Collins, the Shropshire County Archivist, and Gill Oliver from Burton on Trent both provided obscure information for which I was most grateful. As ever the librarians at Eastbourne Central Library never flinched in the face of my constant demands and queries.

Finally, my thanks go to my old friend David Riddick of Crawley, who did some essential checking for me on aspects of the Crawley poltergeist case.

If I have inadvertently omitted to mention anyone I do apologise.

A FRIEND IN NEED

'S-T-E-P- ...' The glass tumbler lurches across the table. '... H-E-N-Y-O-U ...' It zigzags from letter to letter. '... N-G ...'

It's his name. Stephen Young. They thought it would be. It's answered the question.

It? It's answered the question?

It's not 'it' who's answered. Harry Fuller, that's who's answered. Go on, Harry. Tell us more.

Their hands rest on the tumbler as it picks out more letters.

'... D-O-N-E-I-T.'

That's it. That's what Harry's telling them. He says 'Stephen Young done it'. Harry says that. Harry from beyond the grave.

Another question? 'Ask him how.'

And the answer spells out:

'Shot – a shotgun and a pistol'

Get him to say why he did it. Ask Harry why. Why did Young shoot him?

'For money – £6300'

And then comes the last message:

'Tell the police – vote guilty tomorrow'.

And then the four of them put away the makeshift alphabet and the glass. Time for bed.

And the next day, at Hove Crown Court, Stephen Young is sentenced to life imprisonment for the murder of Harry Fuller and Nicola, his wife of only six months.

It's only a matter of weeks before the *News of the World* gets the story. A juror who was there says that four of them improvised an ouija board in the Old Ship Hotel at Brighton. They conjured up the spirit of Harry the victim, who confirmed that Young was the murderer. Good to be reassured that they had reached the right verdict. They'd had a drink or two after a long day in court. Being sent to spend the night in a hotel with a bunch of strangers was like being marooned on a desert island. The only thing they had in common was the murder. So they had this idea of a seance. Saw no harm in it.

But the lawyers did. Young's solicitor claimed that the jury had arrived at their verdict 'not on the basis of evidence but on conversations with the deceased' and he launched an appeal while the Crown's legal team tried to pass it off as 'a drunken experience'. After consideration the Court of Appeal ordered a retrial. The whole seemingly endless, agonising business had to be gone over yet again.

It was months earlier, on 10th February 1993, that Nicola's father had rung the police. He'd been trying to contact her all day at her home in Wadhurst and could get no reply. He wondered if they would just check that everything was all right. But when the police went to the white-painted, three-bedroom Blackman's Cottage they were horrified at the sight which met their eyes. There were two corpses.

Harry Fuller lay downstairs. He had been shot in the back by a single .22 bullet. From the upstairs landing, a trail of blood led to the master bedroom, where Nicola was sprawled. She had been shot four times in the face with the same gun. Her injuries were horrific. It was apparent that the first three bullets, fired on the landing, had not killed her but one of the bullets had passed through her mouth, tearing her tongue. For some reason, probably because he believed her dead, her murderer must have left her and she had crawled into the bedroom. He had then returned to find her still alive and had killed her with a fourth shot.

It was clear to the police investigators that the murder had taken place at around breakfast time – Fuller's suit, Nicola's dressing gown, a coffee cup on the landing. Then, there were other signs: the house had been searched. Desks, cupboards, drawers were disturbed. Somebody looking for something. But what? There was a thin layer of white powder over and round the dead man's body. Was this a drugs deal gone wrong? What did seem certain was that the killings had been carried out quickly and efficiently. But who would want to murder such a decent, well-liked woman as 27 year old Nicola? She was a quiet, unassuming sort. It was inconceivable that anyone would want to kill her.

But Harry, well, he was an altogether different prospect. For Harry was well-known. He was likened to TV's 'Arthur Daley', though it is doubtful if he was quite so genial a character. And he was certainly a better businessman than the hopeless Daley. Harry Fuller was wealthy and he liked people to know it, always taking thick wads of notes out of his pockets. He used to boast that he had £5 million stashed away. He would brag about the Porsche that Jack Nicholson had given him. That was not wholly accurate, of course. Whilst he had such a car, the role played by the generous film star was sheer embroidery. Such a loudmouth, Harry Fuller. Used to play guitar with Wings – so he said.

Detective Superintendent Graham Hill, head of Sussex CID, knew about Harry Fuller. He described him as 'an exaggerator who lived in a larger-than-life world ... If he had £3,000 in his pocket he would tell you that he had £30,000. If he had one Rolls Royce, he would tell you that he had five ... If he rented a house, he would tell you he owned it ... In the end it was Harry's exaggeration that got him killed.'

So, tales of off-shore accounts, friends in high places, acquaintance with the Krays, poured into his listeners' ears. Not bad for a boy who could scarcely read or write, who had little more than the gift of the gab and an eye for the main chance. Not bad for a boy of gipsy stock who'd made his fortune as a dodgy builder, as a rip-off merchant, as a roofer whose shoddy work after the great storm of 1987 annoyed many householders around Crowborough, and as a second-hand car dealer in the Tunbridge Wells area. Now he was 'Flash Harry', ladies' man, big car owner, fancy suit wearer. Some found him engaging. But there were enemies. Not small-time enemies either. Not the resentful few in Wadhurst who stuck pencilled notes on his windscreen with complaints about how he parked his cars. Harry Fuller had more to worry about than a few villagers' gripes about parking.

What emerged in the course of the police enquiries was that Harry now lived in fear of his life. These days he took extreme safety precautions, changing his telephone number two or three times a year. He would never answer the door before checking through the window who was calling. And now the thrice married Harry, 45 years old, was concerned for the safety of his young wife. A business associate, Jeffrey White, commented, 'He told me that he had a chequered past and there might be some people who wanted to know where he lived. He thought there might be individuals who might want to make a name for themselves by attacking him.'

It certainly looked like a grudge killing. But by whom? Diaries and address books found in the house were filled with telephone numbers and addresses of dealers, motor traders, market stallholders, builders, jacks of all trades. Not all were reputable. This was a cast-list of criminals, men and women guilty of deception, theft, robbery, violence. Some had committed major crimes. If there was a crook in the county, then Harry Fuller knew him. It could be any one of these.

Before the enquiry became bogged down, there were three interesting clues. The first was that the white powder round Fuller's body was neither heroin nor cocaine. It was sucrose. Did this suggest that whoever had slain the Fullers was trying to trick the police? If so, wasn't it a rather inept attempt?

More important was the information from the local telephone exchange where all 999 calls were recorded. On the morning of the murder the operator had taken an emergency call at 8.43 am but all that she could make out were muffled, incomprehensible sounds. For more than six minutes, the operator believed she was talking to a very young child. 'Is Mummy there?' she can be heard saying.

On the tape there are sounds of doors opening and shutting, drawers, too, most probably. There is the sound of footsteps, of someone walking downstairs, of a phone receiver being lifted. This someone presumably hears Nicola's plaintive call for help on the upstairs extension, for there is then the sound of feet going back up the stairs. There is a last squeal for help on the tape. Then the receiver is replaced. And still the operator, not unnaturally, thinks she has heard a child at play. She does not raise the alarm. She has heard other children doing exactly this, pretending to use the phone.

Harry and Nicola Fuller on their wedding day (Today *newspaper*)

Then, there is the answering machine. It is in record mode. A man called Steve rings on the night before the murders. He makes an appointment to see Fuller the next morning. Probably it is the killer but all of the Steves in the address book have alibis.

Nine weeks after the murders the case is aired on the BBC *Crimewatch* programme. The voice of Steve is relayed across the nation. The following morning Stephen Young, a 35 year old insurance broker, asks to speak to detectives. He tells them that his sister had heard the TV programme and thought that she had heard her brother's voice. She had advised him to clear the matter up.

But Stephen Young was not unknown to the police investigating the Fuller murder. They had already spoken to him. He had previously contacted them and had made a statement. As a professional man he had thought it wise to tell them that for several years he had looked after Fuller's insurance. He thought it advisable to volunteer himself so that he could be eliminated from the investigation. Fact was, he told the police, he had not seen Fuller for a week before his death. His story was accepted.

But now, Young said, the *Crimewatch* programme had jogged his memory. Of course he had telephoned Fuller, he said, to make an appointment. He should have remembered. It would be his voice on the answer machine. He had gone to Blackman's Cottage on the morning of the murder but there had been no reply. He had then gone back to his car and driven away. He had not been in the village for more than a few minutes.

At this point the police must have felt sure that they had found their man. Not that there was any conclusive proof.

But one of the High Street banks at Wadhurst had installed security cameras. When the film of the morning of 10th February was inspected, there was Stephen Young's car passing by sometime after 8.30 am. And there it was again passing by ... about an hour later. But Young had told detectives that he had been in Wadhurst for only a few minutes.

Motive? The police looked into his finances. Stephen Young, in a responsible and well paid profession, regarded as a successful businessman, was in debt to the tune of £170,000. He had remortgaged his home and now there were threats to repossess it.

Stephen Young (Today *newspaper*)

Credit card firms and insurance companies were pressing him. He owed money to relatives and friends. Yet, on 11th February, he paid £6,300 into his own bank account.

This was Stephen Young, pillar of the community in Pembury, where he lived. This was the married man with two children, the local Freemason, the man who had been only days before the murders the star of the annual local pantomime, where this year he had been so admired for playing the part of the comic arch-villain with such gusto.

And this was the man whose hoard of firearms astonished the police. He was admittedly a member of the 21st Kent Home Guard Rifle Club but what was found in the house was incredible. Not only were there legitimate weapons but also a pump-action shotgun, a self-loading carbine, a sawn-off shotgun, an imitation machine gun, a high powered rifle, a dozen handguns, a grenade launcher, bayonets, machetes, and, in addition, thousands of rounds of ammunition, some of which matched those which killed the Fullers. Strapped under the bed of one of the children was a loaded pistol. And there was more: there were combat jackets, wigs, masks and false MOD number plates. 'There was enough to fill a medium sized room,' one policeman said.

Why such an armoury? What did Stephen Young intend? He never said. Was there more to come? Something worse?

At his trial Young claimed that when he went to the Fullers' home, he found the front door open and so he entered. They were already both dead, he said. He walked outside and saw a shadowy figure at the bedroom window. He fled. He did not contact the police because he had received threatening phone calls.

But his plea was unacceptable. The jury declared him guilty. They knew that Young had made the appointment, that Harry Fuller had opened the door to him. Of course he did. He trusted Young. He led the way into the room where he was shot, all the time with his back to his murderer. Stephen Young was given two life sentences.

And then came the revelations about the ouija board.

At his second trial, Stephen Young was again found guilty. What surprised so many was that this rather handsome businessman could have committed such appalling murders. This was Stephen the Freemason, Stephen the insurance broker, the actor, the family man, the chap who took the local children for football practice. Nor could many understand how he had found it possible to attend a business lunch only three hours after the killings, how that same evening he had felt able to attend a lodge meeting. This was Stephen, 'a good bloke', 'fun to be with'.

It all seemed so wrong. It was incomprehensible to those who thought they knew him. It was not the Stephen that they knew. But did they know him? Was the real Stephen Young kept deeply hidden? Did most people know only the surface Stephen Young? Detective Superintendent Graham Hill was to describe him as 'the most cool and cold-blooded criminal I have known in 25 years of policing'.

Surely that was the real Stephen Young.

THE HAUNTED BEDROOM

L ook at the photo. Look at the boy. He lies in his bed, his wrists bound. He cannot move his hands far on either side. The room is sealed and nothing has happened yet. But it will. It so often does. And on the other side of the door others are waiting too.

It had begun a year earlier in August 1944 when he was eleven. One night there was an air-raid alert. Guns thundered at enemy aircraft in the skies above Crawley. At her bungalow in Woolborough Road, Mrs Rhodes hurried her grandson Alan into the Morrison air-raid shelter in her bedroom. Sometimes there were long silences, broken at times by sporadic fire and the menacing drone of enemy planes; then there were bouts of fierce explosions, though whether from falling bombs or aircraft shells was unclear. Alan and his grandmother curled up in blankets, trying to sleep through the noise and the threat above them. But so often, just as they were drifting off, more dull crumps and thuds roused them. And there were other sounds intruding too. Certainly not guns. More a light, insistent tapping on the metal roof and sides of the indoor shelter. Neither the boy nor his grandmother could make it out, for when the all-clear went they searched the room and indeed the bungalow for a possible cause. In the end they supposed it must have had something to do with the raid. Something had perhaps been dislodged. Something to do with the water pipes or the electricity. Nevertheless, though they told themselves that there must be some obvious explanation for the tapping, they returned to their beds less than convinced.

And the next night, and the night after that, and most nights in the ensuing weeks, the tapping on the shelter continued. Mrs

Rhodes finally became so exasperated that she had it taken out. She would rather risk German bombs than listen to the tap-tap-tapping which so plagued her and her grandson. But that had no effect, for the tapping now resumed on the walls and the beds. And there were other sounds too: bangings, scratchings. It was all beyond explanation. And other things occurred. Doors were unexpectedly found locked. Bedclothes were whipped away during the night. Curtains were taken down and piled in the middle of unoccupied rooms. And one night as he lay in bed, Alan felt a sharp slap on his face.

All this bizarre activity. Mrs Rhodes had never experienced anything like it in her life but she did recognise that whatever was occurring seemed to centre round her grandson. Nothing ever happened when he was out of the house. Most often, it was after he went to bed that the activity commenced Once he was tucked in the noises would begin. Anxious, Mrs Rhodes slept with Alan but whenever she did the bedclothing was pulled off and thrown on the floor. All sorts of objects flew around: keys, pictures, pencils and even a pair of scissors. It was not Alan who was responsible for any of this. Mrs Rhodes had no doubt about that. Whatever was happening in the bungalow had nothing to do with him. In fact, she believed that these unpleasant events were directed against him. For instance, his bicycle was moved from the shed in which he kept it. Another time the door was padlocked. Then, the shed was locked and the key hidden. It seemed so unfair on the child. Often he was late for school because of all of this tampering. And to add to the increasing confusion of their lives, the clocks were frequently altered.

Why did they not report this strange situation? Why did they just try to cope without seeking help? Perhaps the most convincing explanation is that this was happening at a time when people's attitudes were different from nowadays. It would not have been 'normal' to admit to having such curious psychic manifestations. What might people think if they suggested that there was a poltergeist in the house? That there was something wrong with them? And so Mrs Rhodes and her grandson stuck it out.

Over the months they became less afraid of their visitor and instead became angry at his intrusion into their home. They gave him a name: 'Spooky Bill'. And they learnt certain things about him. They knew his noisy times and the times when he tended to leave them alone. They used not to go to bed until after midnight because usually the activity occurred before that. Whilst they could not guarantee a peaceful night when they went to bed late, they certainly had a better chance of undisturbed sleep. They knew too that he liked fire. Sometimes the grate was laid with logs and coal and then a fire lit. On more than one occasion, the gramophone was turned on in the empty sitting-room. Once the gramophone was moved from the sitting-room to the kitchen. And once, there was a note in a childish script: 'Play the Gram or Truble, Love, George.' And when they ignored this demand, there was another note for them. It was simple and brief: 'Truble, see.'

Poltergeists are so often petty and malicious, so often like a particularly unpleasant child. 'Spooky Bill' was no different. He seemed wilful, selfish. Even though Mrs Rhodes and Alan were emboldened to write and to speak to him, asking him to leave them in peace, their requests were ignored. There was always some new inconsiderate behaviour to contend with. At last Mrs Rhodes consulted a spiritualist. Could it possibly be the spirit of Mrs Rhodes' father, the spiritualist wondered. He had died in the bungalow. Mrs Rhodes was doubtful. Her father would never have behaved in such a spiteful fashion. Nevertheless, she asked Alan to write a note asking 'Dear Grandad, What do you want? What can we do for you?'

The next morning they found the note with the word 'Grandad' crossed out.

Despite the fact that they had become accustomed to 'Spooky Bill', his constant presence caused them such anxiety that for three weeks they moved out of the house in the hope that on their return he would have decamped. But when they came back things were no different. He was waiting for them. Would they never be rid of him?

Eventually, Mrs Rhodes' son wrote to Harry Price, at that time Britain's most eminent psychic scholar, and explained the dreadful happenings in his mother's haunted bungalow. In late 1945, after so long a torment, Price came to Woolborough Road to investigate. He was accompanied by the Rector of Pulborough, a journalist, Sydney Jacobson, and a photographer, Ken Hutton, from the magazine *Picture Post*.

Price's first question on arrival at the bungalow was to ask if either Mrs Rhodes or Alan had read his book *Poltergeist over England*. It was not vanity which led him to put the question. He wanted to know if some kind of fraud was being perpetrated. Had they cooked up some tale based on events he had so graphically described in the book? Neither had read it.

At about ten o'clock the investigating team began their arrangements for the night. First the room, which had two beds, a single and a double, was thoroughly searched. Beds and bedding were inspected. Next, the windows were taped so that no one could enter without breaking the tapes. Two small vases were placed on a marble-topped wash-stand and ringed with chalk. Around the base of the wash-stand Price sprinkled chalk, which would reveal if anyone had come near it. Photographs were taken of the dressing table and chest of drawers so that there would be evidence if they were moved. The light was turned out and the room was left empty. On the other side, the door was sealed with tape. After this everyone, Price, the Rector, Mrs Rhodes and Alan, the journalist and the photographer sat down to await developments.

After nearly an hour nothing untoward had occurred. Price told the others that poltergeists sometimes refused to respond when they were being investigated. On the other hand, they seemed very often to be exhibitionists. He said that he intended to challenge the poltergeist in the hope that he might be unable to resist indicating his presence. 'Now, entity, or Spooky Bill, or whatever you like to be called, we have come a long way to see what you can do and we hope that you won't disappoint us. Please give us some manifestation, preferably by moving the vases on the wash-stand.'

There was no response. Price now decided to see if Spooky Bill could be persuaded to respond to music. He put a record of *San Fernando Valley* on the gramophone. Still no response. And when

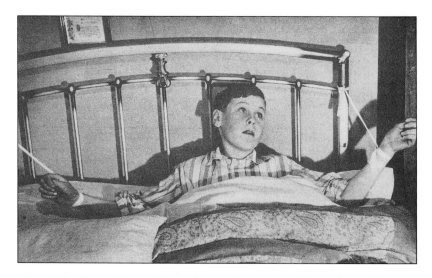

Alan Rhodes, tied to his bed, awaits a visit from the poltergeist
(*Ken Hutton,* Picture Post)

they opened the bedroom door half an hour later, everything was still in place.

After this, the time now about 11.20 pm, Alan went to bed. His wrists were bound and the tapes then tied to the bed rails. It was impossible for the boy to slip off the tapes from his wrists for Price had tied them tightly. He could move his hands for 18 inches or so. His left hand was near the door and he was instructed to knock if anything were to happen.

Within a minute of Alan's being alone there came a knock on the door. When Price and the others went into the bedroom the youngster told them that something had just been thrown. It had narrowly missed his face and had hit the wall. Sydney Jacobson found a small rubber ball on the floor. It had not been there previously. On Alan's bed they also found two pieces of a jigsaw puzzle. Alan told them that he had been constructing the jigsaw earlier in the day but that he had collected up the pieces and had put them back in the box in the sitting-room. The box was later found where the boy said he had left it.

No sooner had they left Alan for the second time than he knocked again. The adults all rushed into the room to find that the tape tying his left hand to the bed rail was unfastened. The tape could not have been pulled loose nor was it cut nor were there any teeth marks on it. Price and the others agreed that it could not have come loose by itself for they had all seen how tightly he had originally tied it. The tape was retied around Alan's wrist and the team retreated outside once more.

In minutes there was another knock on the bedroom door. This time both tapes were untied and had been placed over the bed rail. At that point, something even more eerie happened and yet none of them saw how it did so. The left-hand tape had been tied once more round Alan's wrist, this time in a strange triple knot. Price explained that this was typical poltergeist behaviour. Complete physical changes take place but they are never seen until they are complete. In this instance, first the tape was over the bed rail, next it was tied around Alan's wrist. But no one had seen the tape in other than those two positions.

Both Alan's wrists were then retied and he was left yet again. During the next half hour or so he knocked on the door no fewer than four times. On the first occasion a Meccano key which had been in the kitchen was found on the bedroom floor. An adjustable spanner, again from the kitchen, dropped onto the floor. A candlestick from the chest of drawers appeared on the bed. Then once more Alan's left hand was untied.

Remarkable, this report seems, doesn't it? In defiance of all the laws of physics. Objects cannot move without someone to move them, can they? They cannot fly through walls in such a fashion, surely. And why, one feels entitled to ask, if our poltergeists can perform such remarkable tricks – and they seem no more than tricks – why do they waste their time on such childish things? If they're good enough to defy all physical logic, why don't they do something more sophisticated? But that's it. Poltergeists don't seem to demonstrate much ambition.

Back to the bungalow in Woolborough Road where Alan continues to knock on the door. At about one o'clock the alarm clock, formerly on the dressing table, is on his bed. A quarter of an hour later a trinket case, also from the dressing table, lands on his bed. What is difficult to understand is that the case is full and unlocked. How is it that in its journey to the bed its contents did not spill?

It has been a fascinating night for Harry Price. The Rector of Pulborough agrees that there there are more things in heaven and earth and so on. Sydney Jacobson has a good story and the photographer is delighted with his pictures. It is now about half past one and time to go. Then the house lights go out. Quarter of an hour later it really is time to go and the visitors make for the car. Just as they are about to drive off, Mrs Rhodes comes out into the driveway. She calls out to them that 'things are flying around like mad' and so everyone goes back inside. Yes, it does appear that there have been some moments of madness. Cushions have been thrown about. An electric light bulb which had been on the kitchen table has smashed against the gramophone in the sitting room.

True? Those present thought that they must be. If they were not, who carried them out? Certainly not Mrs Rhodes who had been with the investigators all night. Alan? Did he really have the skill to demonstrate these very typical poltergeist activities? Was he so much of a magician that he could manipulate knots in double quick time? Was he so skilful that he could conceal a rubber ball and pieces of jigsaw until the moment of his choice? Had he some clever way of getting out of bed to move objects from the dressing table? And how did he so cleverly succeed in bringing objects from the kitchen to his bedroom?

Theories to explain poltergeists range from the existence of malicious entities to the unsuspected psychic energies of certain people, especially adolescents. In this case, did Alan, quite unsuspecting of his own powers, release inexplicable energy to cause such havoc to his grandmother and to himself?

Price's visit to Woolborough Road did not stop Spooky Bill. He continued his erratic, immature behaviour for some months more. And then, with no indication of his intentions, he just left. One day there was noise, there were throwings, articles were displaced … and then the next day he went and never returned.

Difficult to give a satisfactory explanation. Perhaps he dropped in on some other poor family. Or was it that Alan's natural adolescent confusions and upheavals settled themselves and that he just grew up? Or are there other as yet undivined reasons for such manifestations?

THE BLUE GARDENIA MURDER

Not difficult to know about Harvey Holford if you were in Brighton in the early 1960s. After all he did win some local fame when in July 1960 he eloped to Gretna Green and then was forced to abandon his plan to marry the girl when her parents made her a ward of court. Not that that stopped them because within months he obtained a High Court order setting aside the injunction. They were married and had a child. Love will find a way, they said.

And there he was, the dashing Harvey Holford, always round the town, in the huge scarlet Pontiac, often with his young wife Christine and their Alsatian, and as often as not towing his motor boat on a trailer. Now that was style. It seemed as if America had come to town. Some people called him 'the King of Brighton' and he had about him enough glamour to be described as 'the Errol Flynn of the South Coast'. Was that because of his way with the ladies? Or was it because he sported such a neat Robin Hood style moustache and short trimmed beard? Or was it because as a club owner he was seen as something special, something rather different from the ordinary run of mankind? Happy chap to have such an envied reputation and a beautiful young wife and a lovely child.

How is it that things sometimes seem to turn so sour?

The Blue Gardenia in Queen's Square was doing well enough. There were gambling tables and drinks; there were interesting people. Admittedly there must have been the usual faded actresses and bent former public schoolboys, along with the bookies and the shady hangers-on cadging drinks, and other fellows with wads of cash from some deal or other. But with its lingering echoes of *Brighton Rock*, that was Brighton clubland at that time, Greeneland staggering to its ultimate conclusion.

Maybe it was because she was too young to settle down. Christine was only 18 when she married Holford. Perhaps he began to seem too old for her, as he was more than ten years her senior. Not that he ever wavered in his love for Christine. But in her case there was some cooling off, though that is not to say that the marriage was in any serious difficulties. Most people would have thought them very happy. But there were odd small incidents. One evening Christine found her husband with one of his former girlfriends. Perhaps she over-reacted. People do from time to time find themselves in the company of former lovers. Then Holford found her kissing Vilasar, one of the barmen at the club. Their association had become blatant and there was in consequence some unpleasantness.

In April 1962 Valerie Hatcher, a 19 year old hairdresser, a friend of the Holfords, went to live at Queen's Square, acting as nanny to baby Karen. Did this denote a lack of maternal instinct on Christine's part? Did it suggest that there were other matters which were more interesting to her than looking after a baby? There was more than a hint that, though nowhere near breakdown, the marriage needed freshening up.

In July, the two girls, Valerie and Christine, nanny and mother, decided to have a holiday in France. Holford, a compliant husband, agreed. Perhaps that would be the answer to the as yet paper-thin uncertainties in the marriage.

But on arrival in France on 12th July, Christine removed her wedding ring. She made no secret to Valerie of the fact that she intended to meet the Swiss, Vilasar, the former barman at the Blue Gardenia. The three stayed in Paris for four nights before moving on to Cannes. Vilasar then left for Nice. Valerie, too, decided to try Nice, while Christine and her latest lover, a German boy called Fritz, went to San Remo. It was here that Christine was told she would have to leave if she brought any more boys into the hotel. Fritz's replacement was Franco, an Italian hotelier, later succeeded by a drummer in Juan les Pins.

Christine and Valerie decided to meet up again in Cannes and it was here, on 8th August, that they renewed acquaintance with

Harvey and Christine Holford (Daily Mirror)

Richard Reader Harris, MP, whom they had met on the beach on their first visit there.

That evening, after dining with Harris, they met John Bloom at the Palm Beach Casino. After this they went to Harris's villa at Cap Ferrat. They had a few drinks and swam in the pool. This was real living for Christine. Holford's club and Brighton could not match this. This was the kind of opulence she had only read about. After this, everything else would seem insipid. Here she was not only with a Member of Parliament but with a young tycoon. Holford could not match this man Bloom who had in the last five years made a huge fortune as head of the Rolls washing machine company. Bloom impressed her with tales of how he had made his millions. He talked about his cars, his private plane and his 60 ft yacht. Harvey Holford with his little club and his absurd scarlet Pontiac could not compare with this.

That night, the one on which they first met, Christine slept with Bloom at Harris's villa.

The next day, Christine, 20 years old, confided in Valerie that she liked Bloom very much. She was very impressed by him. Did Valerie realise that every time Bloom's shares went up by threepence, he made £75,000? And he had made her such an offer. He had promised to give her a flat in Monte Carlo and another in Mayfair. Not that he was offering marriage because he was already married but he would see her regularly, several times a week. And he would give her £20,000 a year. She was seriously considering accepting but first she would have to go back to England to see about her baby and then she would return to France. And Harvey would be all right, she said. If she lived with Bloom she would be able to get enough money to buy No. 5 Queen's Square for him. Christine said that she was going to tell him that. And she had to admit, she told Valerie, 'I have not missed Harvey a bit.'

But back in Brighton, Harvey Holford had begun to fret for the absent Christine. Peter Corvell who managed the Blue Gardenia and Holford's other club, the Calypso, was to say that his boss was 'eating his heart out for her'. In fact, Holford began drinking heavily and lost interest in the business. He kept Corvell up until the early hours at the Gardenia, talking about his fears for his marriage, weeping at what he perceived as his loss. He undoubtedly said to Corvell words to the effect that if he could not have Christine, then no one else would. But perhaps these were just the hopeless words of a desperately worried man.

From time to time, Holford and Christine talked on the telephone. Not that he could always control his temper. What was she up to? When was she coming home? She was now staying at a hotel in Nice, she said. He was less than sympathetic one day when she asked if she could stay longer, in which case she needed some more money. If she had no money, she had better come back, he had answered. Finally, on 11th August, acting on Corvell's advice, at about nine o'clock in the morning, Holford rang Christine. As she assumed that it was Bloom on the line, her confusion must have been apparent when she heard Holford's voice reply to her 'Hello, darling'. Or perhaps, in his anxiety, he did not notice. In any event, he was coming to take her back to England. He would arrive that afternoon.

Holford was to say later that when he arrived in Nice Christine had changed. Everything about her seemed different. Her manner was not the same. Her hairstyle, her dress, had completely altered. She was like a stranger to him. And she told him that she did not wish to live in England any more.

They took a walk around the quayside and she said to him, 'I have met this boy.' Later, she admitted it was Bloom. And she told him about the marvellous offer he had made. Did he not know about Bloom's millions? And she told him she was due to move into the Monte Carlo flat straightaway. And there was the place in Mayfair to be provided by Bloom. Couldn't Holford see what an offer it was? 'If I live with him I will get £20,000 a year,' she said. Couldn't he see how wonderful a deal it was? For both of them?

That night they went to Juan les Pins, visiting nightclubs. Christine drank heavily and was drunk. Holford drank too but stayed sober. Couldn't he see, she asked, if Holford would let her go to Bloom, she could give him the world?

'I do not want the world, I just want you,' Holford replied.

The next day, the Holfords left Nice and went to Majorca, but if they had intended to spend time there they changed their plans for within twenty-four hours they were back in Brighton.

Such arguments now in the flat above the Blue Gardenia, Holford in great rages, Christine defending herself, not seeming to care at times. And then, Holford again pouring out his heart to Corvell. He would do anything to get her back. Should he crash the car and injure himself, he wondered, and thereby arouse her sympathy? And at one point he asked a hypnotist to make him believe that he did not love Christine because there was 'too much pain'. But it all came to nothing.

Shortly after their return Holford found Christine's diary. Several names. Vilasar. Bloom. Others. But it was Bloom's name that most perturbed him. Bloom was the only one who wanted to take her away, the only real rival. Had she slept with him, he asked her for the first time. Until then he had skirted round the question, unable to face the truth, unable to accept what was all too apparent.

But now when she admitted to him that she had been to bed with Bloom and more than once, Holford hit his wife, beat her savagely. And then he cut off her hair. She was completely shorn.

Richard Hughes, Christine's father, said that on 14th August his daughter went to his house at Saltdean. She was almost unrecognisable. 'At the time she was so badly and markedly swollen about the face,' her doctor said, 'that I could not see what was the matter with her nose.' There were red marks between the shoulder blades and neck as though there had been an attempted strangulation.

Holford said that he was deeply sorry and ashamed of what he had done. He had gone on his knees and begged forgiveness. He said that they had had a bit of a row but was sure they would make it up.

Holford had also spoken to his own doctor. Would six tablets kill him, he asked. The doctor told him not to be 'a damned fool' and Holford promised not to take any more. Holford was, however, given a prescription intended to increase his wife's satisfaction. He had been compared unfavourably to Bloom. Apparently he was not really much of an Errol Flynn.

Yet to the proprietor of the coffee bar beneath the Blue Gardenia Holford did sound rather more macho when he said, 'I have cut all her hair off. I have to exert a bit of manliness over her.'

But the truth was that he now tried desperately to heal the breach. He would buy her a new car. Yes, he told her, she could have whatever she wanted. He took her out and about, trying to buy her back.

When Valerie Hatcher, broke, returned to England several days later, Holford met her at Heathrow. Still consumed with anxiety, he pressured her into telling him what had been happening on the holiday. She confirmed that Christine had slept with Bloom. Holford gave her £25 and said he would use what she had told him, and what he had her write down, to sue John Bloom.

On 2nd September, the day after Christine's birthday when Holford had given her a new car, he found a letter from her. She was going to leave him. It read: Dear Harvey, I am going away from Brighton and you. Sorry. It is impossible to forget what happened in Queen's Square. There is something inside me makes me feel very nasty towards you and I cannot go on. One thing I want in life is to be happy.

'In all the time I have known you, you promised me a holiday here, there, and everywhere and the furthest I went was Brighton. It is silly to torture each other like this, so I have made the decision, Harvey. I will always keep in touch with you. I feel so lonely sitting here and am at the crossroads and don't know where to turn. I cannot talk to my father. I am frightened that as the years go on that once a man has hit a woman you can throw everything back in my face and do it again.'

The letter was signed 'Christine' and there was a postscript which plainly said that the baby was to be left with Holford: 'Give all my love to my baby, Karen. I never before felt the way I feel tonight. I wanted so much for us in the beginning. If it had not been for bad manners on both sides we could have succeeded.'

She did not know where to turn, she said, and was afraid he would go on hitting her.

'Every bloody day, every stinking rotten day, she kept mentioning Bloom, the bastard,' Holford later told the court. And now she was going to him.

Now as the days led on to Christine's death, there were the usual arguments, threats, promises to do better.

On the night of 14th September, Holford went to Hove Town Hall to pick up tickets for that evening's Jazz Ball organised by the local press. Early in the evening Christine visited the Warren Country Club at Telscombe Cliffs where she won 15 shillings playing roulette. She then called in at the Montpelier Jazz Club. Later she met her husband, who had earlier been disturbed that she had gone out and had not told him where she was going. They went to the Jazz Ball together after which they called in at the New Hove Albany Club. Then after short visits to the Calypso and the Blue Gardenia they went upstairs to the flat.

There was a row. As usual. Christine said that she was going to Bloom; her hair had grown again. Then she had told him about Karen. She was not his child she told him.

The new nanny, Anthea Harris, had begun work at Queen's Square on 28th August. At about midnight, when she was sitting outside the house in her boyfriend's car, she saw Holford coming out of the Whisky a Gogo Coffee Bar. Later, the manager came over to her with a message. He gave her half a crown and told her to stay away for two or three hours because Holford had a conference in his flat. She did not return until 2.30 am. The lights were on in the flat. She saw Christine's wig on the draining board and it was covered with blood. In the lounge she saw a cardboard box, also covered with blood.

She was a young, frightened girl, uncertain about what she should do. 'I went up the stairs that led to the bedroom and I got about four steps from the top and I was scared so did not go any farther,' she said. 'Then I came back down and switched the light off and went to bed. The next thing I remember is when the police came.'

In the early hours, Holford's mother, who also lived in the flat, saw the bloodied wig too. Frightened, she rang a friend who called the police. They found Holford in bed, unconscious. He wore only a singlet. Christine, fully dressed, was cradled in his right arm and their heads were together. She had been shot six times – three times in the head and three times in the body. He had taken an overdose of drugs. Three days later he was still unconscious in the Royal Sussex County Hospital.

When questioned on 18th September Holford appeared rational but said he could not tell the police anything. Detective

Superintendent Marshall told Holford that it appeared from blood traces that he had carried his wife upstairs from the kitchen and put her in bed, but Holford was uncooperative. He could remember nothing.

Asked about whether he had taken an overdose of sleeping tablets, Holford replied, 'They didn't bloody work anyway.'

When he was told that his wife was shot six times Holford said, 'Completely fantastic. It is completely fantastic. It is just fantastic.'

Then, when the detective asked him if he owned a revolver he answered, 'None that I know of.'

They spoke about Holford cutting his wife's hair. Holford said it was standard treatment in East Germany to cut off the hair of loose women.

'Are you suggesting your wife was loose?' Marshall asked.

'No, not particularly,' Holford replied. 'I just felt like cutting her hair. You don't know how sorry I am. A terrible thing, life, most peculiar.'

But if he was less than helpful to the detective superintendent, Holford was more enlightening to a sergeant left with him in the hospital. 'Briefly,' he told him, 'my wife went to France and had it off with everyone in sight almost. I must have been insane for a while.'

In December 1962, Holford fractured his skull in a fall from the safety wire on the first floor landing at Lewes prison. His trial was postponed until March.

At his trial at Lewes, the prosecution argued that the crime was premeditated and coolly carried out. The defence, on the other hand, pointed to the amount of Seconal that Holford had taken, which would normally have been fatal. Only the early treatment he received had saved him. It had been a genuine suicide attempt by a deeply distressed man. Holford would have died had he not received treatment.

Holford's plea was that he had not planned to kill Christine. Something snapped on the night of 14th September.

Some of the evidence related to Holford's mental condition. He had, according to psychiatrists, a rather abnormal personality. It was his wife's provocation that led to his being unable to control himself the night he shot her.

But why did he have a gun in the house if not to kill her? Then came a most interesting sidelight. Holford had some months earlier written a letter to be opened in the event of his death. It concerned the installation of a Legalite gaming table in the club. He wanted the leasing company to give him a monopoly agreement but was told that for this he would have to pay an extra £4,000. The director of the firm had then mentioned his connections, which included the notorious London gangsters Billy Hill and Albert Dimes. 'If I did not co-operate,' Holford had written, 'something unpleasant would happen to me.' That was the reason for his having a loaded gun in the house. Hill and Dimes specialised in razor slashing.

His statement to the police was read in court and said, 'I tried to show her the error of her ways ... I took her out night after night but it didn't make any difference. All she thought about was money ... that's Bloom for you, the bastard.'

He had gone on to say, 'It is like a dream. How many times I shot her I do not know ... I just wanted to die ... I took all the tablets I could find ... I now regret doing this.'

He went on to tell the court about the improvements he made to the flat. 'I said I was building a palace for my princess.' There was nothing he would not do for Christine.

The jury returned a verdict of manslaughter on grounds of provocation and diminished responsibility. Mr Justice Streatfeild agreed. 'I fully recognise,' he said, 'there must be few men indeed who have been subjected to greater provocation than you were.'

The judge in his summing up commented also on Billy Hill and Albert Dimes, 'Lewes Assizes is not the only place I have sat in my time as a judge. I have sometimes sat at the Old Bailey and those names that appear in that letter were not heard by me for the first time, I assure you ... The thought of having her beauty slashed about with razors was too much for him.' The gun was bought 'against the Billy Hills and Albert Dimes of this world.' It was his opinion that they had a responsibility for the presence of the gun in the Queen's Square flat.

Undoubtedly Mr Justice Streatfeild felt considerable sympathy for Holford, the man who had killed the wife he loved. Christine had told Holford she did not want 'a little house or a little car'.

She knew what she wanted and 'I know how to get it'. She had called Holford 'a little boy'. 'Think of the contempt in those last two words,' the judge said.

Holford was acquitted on the murder charge and on 29th March 1963 was given four years for manslaughter. He was paroled on 2nd October 1964. There is something continental about this, isn't there? It's a crime passionel. It would be better suited to Cannes or Nice, but if it had to take place anywhere in this country perhaps Brighton was most appropriate.

Years later Harvey Holford, the former 'King of Brighton', did step onto the outrageous Brighton scene once again. In February 1974, under the name Robert Keith Beaumont, he stood as independent candidate for Brighton Pavilion in the General Election.

He didn't get in.

A Mysterious Affair

Mrs Madge Knight died in St Richard's Hospital, Chichester on 6th December 1943. She had been admitted four days earlier, suffering from mysterious burns to her back.

Madge Knight, 45 years old, lived at Manor Cottage, Aldingbourne with her husband Herbert, a retired architect. Living with them at this time were Mrs Knight's sister, Sylvia, and her husband, Basil Moore, who had been recently discharged from the Canadian army.

In the early hours of 19th November, the Moores were roused from their sleep by Madge's screams. Her back showed signs of having been severely burned. She never recovered from her injuries nor was she ever able to say how they had come about.

'Some of the features of this case are not entirely satisfactory,' said Mr N. H. Hignett, Chichester District Coroner, following a lengthy hearing at the inquest on 20th December, 1943.

The court heard that on 18th November, Herbert Knight and Sylvia Moore, his sister-in-law, had been to London, coming back about teatime. It was on their return that Madge Knight began an argument with her husband. Basil Moore said she was extremely upset because the day's trip had been wasted: Herbert had failed to secure the election of either Basil or Sylvia to the directorate of the Water Board. Presumably he had some influence over the appointment and had failed to exercise it. Or perhaps Madge had overestimated his powers. Whatever the case, she was incensed, and Herbert, doubtless tired after a day trip to the city, can have been in no mood to put up with her complaints.

At about 7.30 pm the Moores went out for the evening to the pub at Slindon, leaving Herbert to the mercy of his wife. Perhaps they were only too relieved to escape Madge's tirade. As guests in the house, no doubt they felt her rant somewhat embarrassing.

'My wife was very strung up that evening,' Knight told the Coroner, 'and I simply sat in a chair and listened to her. She held forth for about an hour. She was very overwrought.' He seems to have been accustomed to being berated, describing his wife as 'headstrong'. His tactic of simply sitting and listening to her was no doubt one that he found to be effective.

When the Moores got back, Madge was waiting for them. Herbert had just gone up to bed. She was now in a better frame of mind than when they had left her and the three of them had a drink together in the sitting room and followed that up with a drink in Madge's bedroom. This was customary. Madge would usually have five or six whiskies in an evening and then a final nightcap with Basil and Sylvia before retiring. She was in fact a heavy drinker, although her husband was to say that he had very rarely seen her drunk.

At about 11 o'clock, the little party broke up. 'I would not say that she was sober and I would not say that she was intoxicated,' Basil Moore remembered.

Madge usually slept with her husband in the largest of the three bedrooms on the upper floor. But this night she was sleeping in the small spare room.

It was between 3.30 am and 4 am when the Moores were aroused by screams from Madge's room. They scrambled out of bed and went to her. She was lying on her left side, groaning and calling out in great pain. When they threw back the bedding they saw that she wore no pyjama jacket. The skin was peeled off her back, raw, red, angry.

It was inexplicable. The injuries were severe but Madge would not allow them to call a doctor. The Moores were unable to offer much assistance and the record of what they actually did is unclear. It may be that they tried the usual remedies for burns, but it seems from the later evidence that Madge was in too much pain to be given any practical help. After trying to comfort his sister-in-law, Basil left his wife to look after Madge and went back to bed. It was not until 7.30 am that Basil called Dr Sandiford at Felpham.

Imagine the commotion. A woman screaming and two other adults alarmed and excited and wondering what to do. And yet here is a puzzle which was never satisfactorily explained at the inquest. Where was Herbert Knight in all this? And why did they listen to the stricken woman who told them not to call a doctor? Come to that, why was it that the doctor did not turn up till 11 am? Because he had not thought it an emergency, he said. There had been no indication in the early morning call that he had received that this was a serious matter.

In response to the Coroner's enquiries, Herbert Knight said that he had slept soundly throughout the night and had heard no disturbance. When he first learned about Madge's injuries about 8 am he was amazed and could not make out what had happened. He could offer no explanation for what had occurred. There was no coal fire at all in the house, which was lit and heated by electricity. And the question nags – did the others not try to waken him, to tell him of the appalling injuries his wife had suffered?

Three doctors gave evidence in the Coroner's court. Dr Sandiford of Felpham said he did not understand that the first telephone call was urgent but he went about 11 am, in response to a second call, when he was told that Mrs Knight was in great pain. When he arrived he could hear her screaming from the front door. He was shocked at what he saw. He could not examine the wretched woman without administering morphia.

There were extensive burns over the whole of her back and he thought the injuries looked like the natural colour of a straightforward burn. Whatever the cause, the doctor decided, it was a burn though there was no smell of burning nor could he reconcile the appearance of the burns with the electric fire in any of the rooms, none of these had been on during the night.

A Harley Street consultant, Dr H. W. Gordon, who visited Mrs Knight in hospital, said that he asked the patient more than once how it happened but her only reply was that she had nothing to tell him. His examination pointed to the application of some corrosive substance. He could not, however, work out how such a substance could have been applied. He said that he would expect any corrosive liquid to cause damage to soft furnishings.

ALDINGBOURNE WOMAN'S EXTENSIVE BURNS

CORONER'S COMMENTS AT A CHICHESTER INQUIRY

"SOME of the features of this case are not entirely satisfactory," declared Mr. N. H. Hignett, Chichester District Coroner, following a lengthy hearing at Chichester, on Monday.

The inquiry was into the circumstances of the death of Mrs. Madge Knight, 43, of Manor Cottage, Aldingbourne.

The dead woman was the wife of Herbert Edmund Knight, a retired architect and surveyor, of that address. She died on 6th December in St. Richard's Hospital, Chichester, from toxaemia following extensive burns.

The jury returned an "open verdict, owing to the conflicting nature of the evidence."

The husband stated that they were married in September 1934.

rang for Dr. Sandiford about 7.30 a.m.

Supt. Savage: "Have you done away with any clothing or bedding that was in that room that night?"

Witness: "Other than to send the sheets of the bed to the laundry, no!"

Dr. H. C. Sandiford stated that the first message at 8 a.m. was not urgent, and another was received to the effect that deceased was in great pain, at 11 a.m. He heard her screams from the front door. In reply to the jury, the doctor asked deceased how the burns happened, and she replied, "I have nothing to tell you."

Mr. Hugh Walter Gordon, dermatologist, of Harley-street London, said he was called into consultation. He could only hazard an opinion that the injuries were caused by some corrosive liquid.

Newspaper report of the coroner's hearing

Dr Janes, pathologist at the Royal Sussex County Hospital in Brighton, said that, notwithstanding the extensive nature of the burns, the hands were completely free from burns nor was the hair of the head scorched. How strange this was. He was in agreement with Dr Sandiford: a fall on the electric fire could not have produced such burns unless the clothing had become ignited. But there was no sign of any burnt clothing. Then, he thought that Madge could have so injured herself if she had poured a corrosive fluid over her own shoulder while she was in a sitting posture; the sudden intense pain would cause her to throw herself backwards and helped distribute the burns. But was this likely? People do damage themselves but was it likely that she had inflicted such devastating injuries upon herself and then hidden the bottle in which presumably the fluid had been contained? Dr Janes was convinced that the burns had been produced by acid. In the absence of any damage to the bed, he wondered whether the burns might have been sustained in the bathroom.

The police had not been totally happy about the affair at Manor Cottage. They had questioned the occupants about the events of the night but they had all stuck by their story. The police had examined the house and found no evidence of burnt or stained floors, nor was there any sign of burnt clothing or bedding. Nor were there any bottles which had contained acid.

The coroner observed that some features of the case were disturbing. The medical evidence seemed to point to the administration of some corrosive fluid. This could only have been applied by the deceased herself or by someone else and there was no positive evidence whatever either way.

Commenting on the inquest, the *West Sussex Gazette* described the case as 'one of the most baffling combinations of circumstances which a Coroner could have to investigate'.

The jury found a verdict on the lines of the medical evidence but left it open as to how the burns were sustained. The mystery has never been satisfactorily resolved.

All these years later, the death of Mrs Madge Knight still remains a puzzle. And it is unlikely now that it will ever be resolved. Harry Price, the celebrated psychic investigator, did not rule out poltergeist activity. As he said, poltergeists were known to start fires and their possible influence here should not be discounted. Michael Harrison who studied the matter of spontaneous human combustion over many years was in no doubt that Mrs Knight had fallen victim to that seemingly most irrational form of death. The evidence of the medical men with their suggestion that she had had acid poured over her, he dismissed as absurd. In his view, Madge Knight died as a result of spontaneous human combustion and this the medical men could not, would not, countenance. And Jenny Randles and Peter Hough, serious scientific investigators into SHC, include the case of Mrs Knight in their findings on the subject. They do not claim to know that Madge Knight was a victim of SHC but they do acknowledge that the case has certain characteristics of the phenomenon.

Poltergeist? The popular theory is that sometimes an individual's powerful emotional upheaval becomes externalised so that there is a release of energy which is violent, which can move inanimate objects, can appear to throw them around a room, can in some instances begin fires where no obvious source of ignition is present. Was this what happened at Manor Cottage when Madge Knight, now in bed but still incensed by Herbert's failure, released a powerful energy which turned itself on her?

Or what if it was a case of SHC? What if some internal disruption of the gases which we all generate in the intestinal system as a consequence of our diets simply exploded? Was there some internal fire which raged, leaving whatever else might naturally be assumed combustible barely touched?. There are hundreds of recorded cases of a quite inexplicable nature not totally unlike this.

Or was there something else which never came to light?

DEATH OF A POLICEMAN

What are we to make of Dr Edgar Power? He's the real puzzler in this story. Over the years practically nobody who has heard about his part in the Eastbourne murder has had a good word to say about him. He's been described as 'contemptible', 'a Judas' and 'a swine'. Doesn't this seem a shade harsh for a man who helped to bring the murderer of a policeman to justice? One thing is sure: if Edgar Power hadn't walked into the police station at Eastbourne in the late afternoon of 10th October 1912, not 24 hours after Inspector Arthur Walls was shot, the case is unlikely ever to have been solved.

On the evening of 9th October, Inspector Walls was called to Countess Sztaray's house, 6 South Cliff Avenue, where it was reported that a man was crouching on the canopy above the front door. Walls approached the man, asking him to come down. Instead, the Inspector was shot and died within minutes. No one had a good look at the killer. The only clue was a trilby hat, size seven and a quarter, lying in the road.

Within an hour Major Teale, Eastbourne's Chief Constable, had telephoned Scotland Yard. 'We have had one of our Inspectors murdered tonight by a burglar,' his message said. 'Will you please let me have the services of one of your best officers to come down by the first train in the morning?'

Murder in Eastbourne? In 1912? Was it conceivable?

Imagine, a murder in this refined place. Behind the noble seafront with its fine hotels and handsome parades, intersected by superb lawned squares and avenues, lay the houses of the rich and powerful, substantial homes of brick or stone, many of them in impressive terraces, others grandly semi-detached and yet others in their own grounds. They were peopled, these elegant houses, by high ranking retired military and naval men and their families, scores of them – admirals, colonels, lords and ladies, and many others of similar rank and status in these few acres. The town was built for these folk and for the knights and baronets and the countless gentlemen and ladies 'of independent means'. Blackwater Road, Carlisle Road, The Saffrons, Devonshire Place, St John's Road, all had their share of such significant people. Add to these residents many influential members of the legal profession, the more prosperous clergymen, affluent businessmen, retired senior civil servants and it amounts to a very select section of the community. And naturally their children were suitably provided for. There were many schools, all of them established for 'the Sons of Gentlemen' or for 'Girls of Good Social Position'. Supporting these was a huge cast of bit-players – chauffeurs, parlourmaids, nannies, housekeepers, companions and governesses, gardeners, nurses, cooks-general, coachmen, valets and 'girls'.

But the murder of a policeman – it must now have seemed that the barbarians were within the gates. It must have seemed that the long, still lingering Edwardian summer was at last coming to an end.

Shortly after 8 o'clock on the morning after the murder, two experienced Metropolitan Police officers arrived in Eastbourne. One was Detective Chief Inspector Elias Bower, described by his colleagues as 'a rough diamond, one of the old time dicks', who several years earlier had solved the Moat Farm murder. He was accompanied by Detective Sergeant William Hayman, who had been involved in the Crippen case.

The detectives spent the day inspecting the crime scene and interviewing witnesses, only one of whom had managed even a brief glimpse of the man on the canopy. Routine investigation but no real lead. And then who should turn up at Eastbourne police station but Edgar Power. He said that he could tell them who the murderer was.

Bower must at first have been impressed by the young man in his early thirties who presented himself with the promise of such remarkable information. He was tall, smartly dressed, well spoken. If what he had to say was useful and true, what a

Chief Inspector Elias Bower

splendid witness he would be. Bower knew that appearances mattered in the witness box. Put up in the box a man who was presentable, who was articulate and confident, and the jury would take little convincing that his account of matters was accurate. And if he was a professional man, a doctor, so much the better.

Power told the detective that he had information but that he must insist that any part he played in the investigation must not be made public. This was absolutely essential, Power said. Could he rely on the Chief Inspector's discretion, he wondered. It was rather delicate. If Bower had any misgivings about this, he kept them to himself. What mattered to him was clearing up the case.

Power knew the identity of the murderer, he said. It was a friend of his, John Williams, a professional housebreaker. Williams had a revolver, had sworn never to be taken alive and had talked about burgling the Countess's house.

There followed an explanation of the whole train of circumstances which had led the doctor from London to Eastbourne. He lived in Finsbury Park where he had rooms in the same house as his business partner, John Mackay. That morning a letter had arrived for Mackay, posted in Eastbourne just the evening before. Mackay had shown Power the letter. It was an urgent call for help sent by Williams. As far as he could recall, it read something like: 'If you will save my life, come down to 4 Tideswell Road, Eastbourne, and bring some cash with you. Urgent.' Almost immediately, both men had an idea of what had occasioned the letter. They had already read about the Eastbourne murder in the newspaper.

Power agreed to accompany Mackay to Eastbourne and the two men caught the 1.27 pm train from London Bridge, arriving in the town in mid-afternoon. After giving Power a couple of sovereigns to pay any bills that Williams might have, Mackay had gone to the Royal Hotel, leaving his companion to go to Tideswell Road, where Williams was staying with his lover, the exquisitely beautiful 21 year old Florence Seymour, who at the time was seven months pregnant and frequently ill.

Mrs Emily Mann, who let rooms at this address, was later to recall a man in a frock coat and top hat calling in the middle of the afternoon. 'It was a man who I thought was a doctor. He looked like one,' she said. He had asked for Mrs Seymour. This rather disconcerted her: the couple staying with her were called Sinclair but then Williams came to the door. Perhaps she had misheard, she told herself. 'How's the wife?' she heard Power say. 'I heard she was rather queer. I thought I'd run down and have a look at her.'

Once Mrs Mann was out of the way, Power challenged Williams, asking him if he had had anything to do with the murder. Of course he had not, Williams told him. But a man with his record could not afford to hang about in a place where such a crime had been committed. The police would be sure to pick him up. It was urgent that he get away to London. Power told the Chief Inspector that he had tried to persuade Williams to stay where he was. He had told him that if he was innocent he had nothing to fear but the very fact of running away to London was likely, if ever it came out, to look suspicious.

Now, at Eastbourne police station, Power told the detectives that he had just seen Williams and Mackay off on the London train and that he had agreed to go back to Tideswell Road to pick up Florence, and escort her to London separately. Power promised Bower that the next day he would get in contact and lead him to Williams.

'Such information,' Bower wrote, 'coming as it did from a man who purported to be a reputable medical practitioner, created a very unfavourable impression but I was positive that this man knew more than he had told us.'

Unfavourable? Well, he must have puzzled, how did this man, a member of such an esteemed profession, know a housebreaker, a possible murderer, so intimately? But Bower had not raised too many questions, aware that if he did so Power would remind him of his conditions. So the curious question, for example, of John Mackay and his connection with Williams was not answered. For the moment, putting aside these queries, the Chief Inspector was grateful to know so early in his investigation that he had a very promising suspect. These other matters would have to wait.

That night Dr Power escorted the fretful Florence to London. The following morning, Power telephoned Williams and they arranged to meet at Moorgate railway station. They were settling down for a drink when at midday the police came in and arrested the unsuspecting Williams.

Property in Williams's lodgings included jewellery, two hats size seven and a quarter, a false moustache, a gun holster and several pawn tickets, providing material enough to convict him of burglary. The pawn tickets related to jewellery stolen during several visits during the summer to Bournemouth and Eastbourne, where Williams had burgled houses in Grassington Road, Saffrons Road and St Anne's Road.

At 6 Bolton Road, a house in which Williams and Florence had previously lodged in the name of Seymour, the landlady, Mrs Daniels, had noticed among their luggage, a violin case – stolen, as it happens. 'In consequence of seeing the violin case,' Mrs Daniels observed, 'I thought perhaps he was a musician and seeking a post at the Devonshire Park Orchestra or that he was a gentleman's superior servant. I knew that he was not a gentleman.' So she speaks to us from a past much more sensitive to the acute gradations of class and status than today. Or perhaps she spotted the tattoo – drums and flags – on her lodger's wrist.

Bower knew that his evidence for murder was thin. What he needed was Williams's gun, which he was sure had been hidden or thrown away. He was certain that Florence must know where it was. In the succeeding days, responding to the detective's urging, Edgar Power found out from Florence that on the morning after the murder Williams had buried the gun on the beach. Now the doctor told her that she ought to return to the beach, find the revolver and hide it in a safer place. On 15th October, six days after the murder, they went together to Eastbourne, all the time shadowed by police. When Florence failed to find the gun in the sand, Bower picked her up at Eastbourne railway station and took her in for questioning. Unaware of Power's role, she believed that he too was under arrest.

It was after midnight when Sergeant Hayman, working by torchlight, found the revolver in the sand and pebbles near the redoubt where Florence had been searching earlier in the day.

At the police station, Florence, desperate about her situation, troubled about her lover, was genuinely ill. The subtle Bower left her alone with her friend, the doctor, who, over a period of four hours, persuaded her to make a full confession. It was damning. Eventually, at about midnight, the sick girl told how at about 7 o'clock on the night of the murder she and Williams had sat at the top of South Cliff Avenue, how he had left her for thirty minutes, how he had returned without his trilby.

In the succeeding days, Bower turned up other information which was not revealed until after the trial. The 29 year old Williams was in reality George Mackay, brother of John. Throughout his life, he had been in trouble with the police. He had been court martialled and dismissed from the Coldstream Guards; he had served several prison terms. And John Mackay and his sister begged that their brother's identity should not be publicised because they said it would break their father's heart. Their father was in fact a Presbyterian minister in Kincardineshire. So Williams was tried under his assumed name, one of the several he used.

Sometimes John Williams is referred to as 'the hooded man'. Bower insisted that he come to court with a blanket over him and that no photographs should be taken of the accused man. As ever, the press managed to ignore the injunctions. Bower had hoped that a witness might be able to identify Williams as the man on the canopy. As it turned out, no one at the three identity parades held at the police station ever identified him as the man who shot Inspector Walls.

In the weeks before the trial John Mackay, anxious about his brother, tried to make Power, who was to appear for the prosecution, change his testimony. He enlisted Walter Townsend, a professional boxer, pimp and thief, to make Power say that Williams's gun had been incapable of firing and that Williams's trilby was of a different size from that found near the murdered man. But Townsend's threats – 'I'll kick your face in if you don't say what I tell you'- did not work. Power held out, appeared in court, and stood up to severe questioning. Though the judge and jury clearly despised Power for what they perceived as his treacherous behaviour, they could not ignore the weight of his testimony.

Then Florence retracted her confession. She told the court that when Bower questioned her, she had been confused about the date; she had been ill; he and Power had badgered her for hours. And, late in the day, and not until he took the stand, Williams introduced into his defence the fact that there was another gang of London thieves in Eastbourne at the time of the murder. He had spoken to them, he said. But it was all too late.

The jury found John Williams guilty in less than thirty minutes. Nevertheless, it is unlikely that such a train of circumstantial evidence would have produced the same verdict today.

The trial was notable as the first occasion on which photographic ballistics evidence was presented to a jury but even though the fatal bullet was proved by Robert Churchill, the ballistics expert, to have similar rifling to the bullets he tested in Williams's revolver, he could only say that it came from a similar type of gun. He could not swear that the gun he had tested was that which fired the bullet.

As for the trilby hat, which certainly was sold in a shop in Bournemouth in the summer when Williams was there, there was no proof that he had purchased it. Though larger than average, it would have fitted one in twelve men.

A rope, ideal for housebreaking, had been found on the beach and Williams did not deny that he had thrown away a rope but that, he said, was on the evening before the murder, when he did admit to having been in South Cliff Avenue. At the time of the murder, he told the court, he had been at 'a picture palace' in Seaside. And whilst nobody could say they had seen him there, nobody had seen him in any other location at the crucial time.

Florence bore a girl, whom Williams was allowed to hold the day before he hanged. He put a piece of prison bread into the baby's hand. 'Now,' he said, 'nobody can say your father gave you nothing.'

But back to Power. How should we regard him? He did betray both Williams and Florence. Some say that this was because he wanted Florence for himself. Others favour a different explanation. They say that only days before the murder Williams threatened to shoot him after an argument. When Power realised what Williams was truly capable of, he went to the police.

In the course of the investigation, Chief Inspector Bower, that wily old fox, had gradually learnt more and more about the useful

The prisoner, John Williams, in the dock

Dr Power. He found out that he was not a doctor. Nor was he an Edgar, nor a Power. He discovered he was really Duncan Brady, ex-public schoolboy, ex-medical student, failed businessman and ex-convict. Just prior to the murder, he and Williams had been to see that other old fraud Horatio Bottomley, the proprietor of *John Bull* magazine, who incidentally lived at The Dicker, outside Eastbourne. Would he, they asked, be interested in a juicy story about a Tory MP? Truth is that Williams and Power had just failed in an attempt to blackmail the parliamentarian. Perhaps they could squeeze some money for the story out of Bottomley. But he was not interested.

But Bower, having all of this information, was able to exercise increasing influence over the phony doctor. So how should we feel about this Dr Edgar Power, who in the immediate aftermath of the trial left the country? As 'a swine'? 'a Judas'? Was he really so 'contemptible'? This chap who returned later to a renewed life of crime has not very much to commend him. Should we then side with those eminently respectable folk who condemned him as a cad? This chap ratted on a friend, they say, he deceived a girl. Or should we think differently about a man who helped to bring the killer of a policeman to justice?

It's a puzzle.

Oh, and Florence? They say that her baby was adopted and that she, who had so deeply loved her executed lover, returned to London's underworld.

But that is only hearsay.

APPARITIONS AT AMBERLEY VICARAGE

Most parents seem to understand. When one of their young children announces a very special friend they are usually ready to enter into the world of imagination, to exchange gossip about the unseen friend's wonderful qualities: 'He lives in a castle', 'Her mother is a fairy', 'He can run, jump etc farther than anyone else', 'She is kind and takes me to tea'. And the parents smile, nod, express pleased surprise that their child has such a marvellous companion. All imagination, of course. Or is it?

Sometime around 1900, the little girl Noel Streatfeild, later a well known children's author, had a friend of about seven years old who used to play with her in the vicarage garden at Amberley, where her father, later to become Bishop of Lewes, had his first living. Despite having a younger sister and brother, Noel played most often on her own and it was at the rose tree in the garden – one which bore both red and white flowers – that she most often met the little girl with the long gold ringlets and wearing a crinoline and pantalettes. Yet Noel never mentioned the little girl to her parents. But then, some girls can keep secrets. And so can little boys and it may be, though it is not certain for the evidence is conflicting, that her younger brother and sister also saw the little girl. But the parents certainly heard nothing from either of them about the child who came to play in their garden.

But if the Streatfeild children kept silent about their little companion, their parents were most certainly aware that their home was haunted by the apparition of a girl. How could they not be? Even if they never saw her, the servants knew of the haunting and so did the locals.

Doesn't it seem remarkable that the Rev Streatfeild and his wife chose to ignore the presence of a ghost? It has been suggested that the Streatfeilds did not know of the supernatural happenings in their home but that is untenable. Why else did so many relatives come to stay with them and yet never pay a return visit? One of them, in fact, left before breakfast after enduring just one frightening night in the spare room. Relative after relative from their large families came to visit, only to experience something unpleasantly uncanny. Not that they ever saw anything but the visitors were aware of a presence. Once they were in bed the door handle would turn and the door would open and then shut. And then it would seem that someone would walk across the room, pausing to look down at the terrified visitors in their beds. This might happen several times a night.

Yet it was never spoken of. Visitors made no mention of any nocturnal happenings and it was only their breakfast-time

Amberley vicarage

tenseness which revealed that they had been disturbed. Doesn't it seem odd that the Rev Streatfeild did not try to come to grips with what was occurring under his roof. Why no attempted release of an earthbound spirit? Was this a case of a young clergyman being unable to face up to the supernatural? It has been suggested that he and his wife kept silent about their ghosts as they believed that mentioning them would deter further visits from their adored families. This does not really sound convincing.

In later years Noel Streatfeild was to reflect on what caused the little girl to appear. She hinted in her short story *The Little Girl* that the apparition came most often when her elder sister, a sickly child who lived most of the time with her grandparents away from the village's damp atmosphere, came to stay. Did her parents fear that it was some quality in their daughter's psychic make-up that raised the ghost of Amberley Vicarage? Was it she who caused the appearance of the little girl?

There were also some poltergeist-type disturbances during the time the Streatfeilds lived at Amberley. Sometimes these are associated with children's psychic disturbances. Did the anxious parents wonder if these too emanated from the sickly daughter who came to stay occasionally with them? Sometimes the little girl had what Noel Streatfeild was later to refer to as 'naughty fits', when she broke kitchen utensils and china. The noise was unbearable and could be heard upstairs. Childish footsteps were heard in the house. But still, in spite of their obvious anxieties, the parents ignored what was painfully obvious to others. Psychology was in its infancy then and perhaps the Streatfeilds were unable to comprehend or to face up to what was a horrifying prospect. But the fact that the disturbances continued after the Streatfeilds, greatly relieved, left Amberley for St Leonards in 1902, suggests that any fears they might have entertained about their invalid daughter' being a cause of the haunting were unfounded.

There was also an old man who used to haunt the staircase. The Stretfeild children saw him at least once, when he wakened them. They screamed for their parents: 'It's the old man, the old man!'

Mrs Ella Carr, who came to the vicarage with her husband, Dr G. F. Carr, was made of rather sterner stuff than her immediate predecessors. She had not believed in ghosts prior to her arrival at Amberley Vicarage. Yet, on the very day of her arrival at the vicarage, there was a girl in a white, short-sleeved crinoline and pantalettes playing on the lawn. The child's hair was parted in the middle and fell in thick fair curls on each side of her face. How odd, Mrs Carr thought, a child in the garb of nearly a hundred years earlier. Perhaps she was coming on an errand from someone in the village. But although she waited long enough, no one knocked at the door. Eventually Mrs Carr sent for one of the servants. No, came the response, no one had called.

Intrigued, Mrs Carr sent for Cook. 'Do come here and look,' the puzzled Mrs Carr said. 'There's the most extraordinary little girl on the lawn. Who is she?'

Cook was able to enlighten her new mistress about the child's identity. She was not fazed in the slightest. In fact she seems to have been quite matter of fact in her explanation.

'Oh, her!' Cook answered, 'That's the ghost. The last vicar and his wife never saw her, so nobody spoke of her, but she's always playing in the garden.'

Cook went on to explain that she regarded the ghost-child as part of the household, though, she said, she was clearer on some days than others. And there was another ghost too, Cook added. A woman. Not that any of the staff ever saw her but they were aware of her. Sometimes they felt her passing on the stairs. She was taken for granted in the kitchen and in fact Cook told how at times she was quite sharp with the ghostly visitor, saying to her when she got in the way: 'Oh, get out of the way, do!' At other times the servants would be aware of this mysterious presence sitting in the same room with them. But they weren't alarmed by her. To them she was just part of the furnishings.

Talking to parishioners Mrs Carr discovered that a similarly dressed child had appeared in nearby cottages over many years, that one night she had even appeared at the end of a woman's bed. Several people expressed surprise that the vicar's wife had never heard of the apparition, as if it were just a normal feature of Amberley life.

The Carrs, despite the girl in the garden and despite the noises they heard in the house, were not alarmed by what they found at

Amberley Vicarage. They were no more alarmed by the apparitions and the nightly sounds than their servants. By 1904 they were well settled in the vicarage when the decision was made to extend the dining room. As a result the old building required quite extensive alterations and it was in the course of these that there was an interesting discovery. Two feet under the dining room cupboard, the workmen came across the skeletons of a woman and child. More bones were found in the kitchen. They were judged to have been buried for about 100 years. Perhaps, the Carrs said, this was why their dogs had not liked going in the kitchen. And it was recalled how the immediate predecessor to the Revd Streatfeild, the Revd Clarkson, who had been at the vicarage for over fifty years, had often complained of smells in the dining room. Drains, he had concluded.

There was a tale of an illicit love affair that people recalled locally. And the murder too of a mother and her child. Clarkson's cook had claimed to have seen the figure of an old man in the house, presumably the figure that later terrified the Streatfeild children. Was this the murderer? And were the woman and child his victims?

This story has an unpleasant end, too. According to Noel Streatfeild the bones were made ready for burial but prior to the service all of them, save the thighs, disappeared. But where? And so one wonders, too, about these friends that so many children speak of so blithely. Are they *all* figments of the imagination?

And finally, one ought to say that the vicarage is still occupied but that the present occupants have experienced no strange happenings.

Poor Widow Woman

'If anyone can help ...' and here Jean's voice falters momentarily before continuing, '... if anyone can give the police any information ...' Her eyes fill with tears and her pain is obvious to the viewers. They know the story, the horror of it, how at midnight her husband, answering the door, had been shot in the heart. He had lain in the passage with the blood pulsing through a massive hole in his chest. Who could not have been horrified by what had happened? Retired bank consultants are not normally gunned down in this fashion. This was like a contract killing, more Hollywood than Northiam. Such a brutal, cruel murder is out of place in such a location, a little Rother village, where venerable old houses look out onto a peaceful green. Small wonder that Jean Daddow is overwhelmed at the memory of what had occurred. She brushes away the tears with a dainty handkerchief and bravely resumes the television appeal ...

What a mystery. Here was an ordinary couple, middle aged, respectable, comfortably off, living in beautiful Chapelfield Cottage. One might have been forgiven for envying them. How was it that they had been visited with such tragedy? How was it that totally out of the blue on 26th November 1991 their world had come crashing down in such a fashion?

The police had arrived to find Jean, a pretty woman in her early fifties, standing by her dead husband, too shocked to give much of a coherent story. They had been in bed, she said, when the bell had rung, and Terry had put on his dressing gown and had gone downstairs. She had heard him unbolt the door, heard him open it, and then she heard the shot. She had run downstairs but had seen no one and there she had stood paralysed with shock at the sight of her husband as he lay dying.

In the first hours after the killing, asked by the police if she knew who might have committed the murder, Jean was able to suggest that although her husband had no enemies she knew a man who might have been responsible. There had been some trouble, she said, about their cottage. They had married, Terry and she, only a couple of years earlier and an old lady, Anne Burton, had bought it for them. Bought their cottage for them? Jean explained that her husband had been able to advise Mrs Burton on her financial affairs and that she had been grateful to him, so grateful that she had bought the £160,000 cottage for them when they married. In her opinion, though she had no proof of this, the murderer was a relative of Mrs Burton. It was an act of sheer jealousy, the desire for revenge, the product of deep resentment.

This lead was quickly followed up. The accused man and his sons were questioned but their alibis were strong. At the time of the murder, the father had been in the company of the former assistant chief constable, and the sons' accounts of their whereabouts were equally unassailable.

Well, Jean told the detectives, when she heard that her suspect was in the clear, she had wondered if her husband might have been having an affair. It might be the work of a jealous husband or boyfriend. And the police pondered that possibility.

But in the first days of the investigation, there were other matters coming to light which persuaded Detective Superintendent Brian Foster to look more closely at the sorrowing widow.

Local people had begun to volunteer information which put a curious cast on the drama. For instance, the door-to-door enquiries raised questions about the time of the gunshot. Northiam at night is normally very quiet and a gunshot is remarked upon. And so, several witnesses were able not only to say that they had heard the shot but that they knew exactly when it was fired. And there was a record too of the time that Jean Daddow made her hysterical 999 call. Why, Superintendent Foster wondered, was there a discrepancy of quarter of an hour between the firing of the gun and the desperate summons for help? But when he asked Jean about this, he was given an answer which perhaps he had anticipated. She had been too distressed to call the police straightaway; she had been in shock, she said. Well, the detective must have mused, she would say that. For now, he had become highly suspicious of Jean Daddow. Was she really a grieving widow, horrified by an atrocious murder on her own doorstep? Or had she some part to play in this awful crime?

More and more bits and pieces came to light as the police garnered their information. For example, only the day before Terry Daddow was killed there was a most remarkable public announcement in a local magazine, *The Wealden Advertiser*, where the following ungainly insert appeared:

DADDOW, TERRY, JEAN. Because of malicious gossip would like it known they are happily married and together. All have been proved by solicitors etc. NOT guilty of fraud, theft or senility. Thanks to the few true friends who believed in us perhaps the rest could find themselves to criticize or work for their sick minds.

Malicious gossip? Fraud? Theft? The police enquiries uncovered stories about how the Daddows had been given their home. It had certainly raised eyebrows locally and there had been whispers. And not only that, there were rumours of other such gifts from other grateful clients. There were even suggestions of dishonesty. Out came the story that the fraud squad and officials from Terry Daddow's own bank, Lloyds, had investigated Mrs Burton's gift. But no charges had ever been brought and indeed Lloyds pronounced its employee to be a man of the utmost probity, a seemingly indispensable servant of the bank. Nevertheless, Terry Daddow, 51 years old when he was killed, was already retired.

And now, the whole respectable front began to unravel. For not only were there whispers of financial dubiety but also tales about the relationship between Terry and Jean. They were not, so rumour said, the sweet and comfortable man and wife team that Jean had spoken of but instead an unhappy, brawling, deeply unpleasant couple. Their two-year marriage, so it seemed, had been crumbling. Nor, according to the stories now circulating, did it appear that one partner was any better than the other. Both appeared to be deeply flawed. There was deceit here, it was said, violence, corruption. The murder of Terry Daddow, people began to say, came out of a sordid, untrusting household.

In 1985 Jean – Mrs Blackman in those days, but divorced from a husband to whom she had been continuously unfaithful, a wife with a string of lovers – went to the bank at Tenterden to talk to someone about her stolen credit cards. And it was Terry Daddow who dealt with the matter, who gave her his undivided attention, and who then conducted an affair with her which was ultimately to lead to his deserting his wife and three children, to a romantic elopement to Gretna Green, to settling down in Chapelfield Cottage.

But there were other stories too that the police picked up. They heard that perhaps Jean, a scheming, selfish woman, was still involved with other men; that Terry, free now from work but depressed, was an alcoholic who beat his wife. Certainly Jean had confided in others that Terry, that reliable Lloyds' employee, was brutal to her and sometimes she had the bruises, the black eyes which proved the truth of what she said. In her diary she wrote that he used her as a punch bag. And in between there was the sex, the kinky letters he wrote to turn her on, the home-made videos.

It was plain to Superintendent Foster and his team that Jean Daddow held the key to the truth. But who had fired the shot? It looked so much like the work of a contract killer. Could Jean Daddow have found someone willing to murder for her?

What about Roger Blackman, her son by her first marriage? He was a 23 year old motor mechanic, suspected of drug dealing and certainly a man who mixed with criminals. Someone told the police that Jean had on one occasion been heard asking Roger if he could find someone to kill Terry. But perhaps it had been said in jest, a playful joke by a married woman. In any case, the police did not think Roger a likely murderer. But was it possible, with his dubious connections, that he knew someone who was?

There was more questioning of Roger's acquaintances. It was said that he dealt in drugs. Did anybody owe him money? Well, there was one chap, Robert Bell, from Headcorn, who had owed Roger money for drugs, several thousands, it was rumoured.

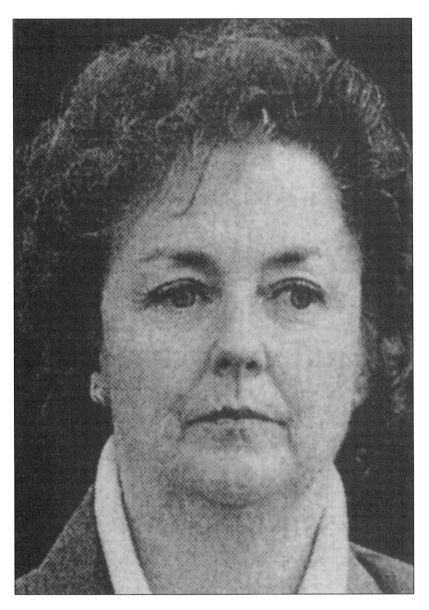

Jean Daddow

Apparently his family had been threatened. It was a case of pay up or else. But he was out of work. Desperate. An ex-soldier. He'd even been in the French Foreign Legion, knew about firearms and explosives and that sort of thing. Certainly worth questioning him, the police thought. He looked possible.

But too late. When they turned up at his door, Bell had gone. Quite suddenly. Left for the United States. But then he was traced. The Sussex police managed to find his whereabouts, managed to get a message to him, told him that they wished to interview him. And just to emphasise matters, they sent a second message to say that if he did not return voluntarily, they would have their good friends in the FBI pick him up and return him to the UK.

And so Robert Bell arrived back in England. But if he had felt confident that he could persuade Superintendent Foster and his team of his innocence, that self-assurance soon deserted him when on landing he was arrested and charged with murder. All at once he wanted to tell everything that had happened, explain the whole dreadful business in which he had been forced to play a part. Not that he had killed Terry Daddow, he said. And the surface-tough ex-soldier poured out the story.

They'd offered him £12,000, Jean and Roger. They'd wanted him to get rid of Terry as fast as possible. They'd hated him, hated his violence, his drunkenness, his moods. They were desperate to be rid of him. They were both after Terry's money. There was the house and cash, lots of it. Jean wanted her hands on that. And furthermore, she wanted to be rid of the man who so ill-treated her. She was tired of it, the beatings, the temper tantrums. It couldn't go on. Bell had just strung them along, pretending that he would kill Terry but really all he wanted was cash to get him out of his money problems. They had handed over several thousand pounds and that was all that mattered to him. They had handed him the money in notes, in a shoebox. It came out of Terry's account so that he was in a way paying for his own murder.

But, Bell insisted, Terry was never really in danger from him. He had deliberately botched several attempts on the man's life. Jean and Roger put it down to incompetence but in reality it was not his intention to become involved in murder. Or so he said. And so Robert Bell talked on and on to the policemen.

Throughout the summer of 1991, the three of them, Jean constantly proposing and urging, had plotted how best it might be done. Not until mid-October, however, was the first attempt made. In all, there were seven attempts to kill Terry, Bell told the police. He had had to play a part, pretending to be serious but all the time considering how eventually he would be able to keep the money and yet escape performing the deed.

If they had not ultimately had such tragic consequences, Robert Bell's abortive efforts to kill Terry Daddow might have been regarded as farcical. Bell claimed that they were deliberately botched by him; perhaps the first two or three efforts were. But certainly they were all as hopeless as they were callous and cowardly. In the end, the inept hitman succeeded but not before some humiliating failures.

On the first occasion, he arrived at the door of Chapelfield Cottage wearing a crash helmet, its visor obscuring his face. He had armed himself with a steel bar. The plan was to ring the bell and when Terry opened the door he was to be bludgeoned to death. Inside, Jean, who had turned off the outside security light, waited for the ring at the bell. Outside, Roger waited in the car. What went wrong? A sound from inside had unnerved Bell and he cut and ran.

On another occasion he shadowed the Daddows on a trip to Devon, where he was to shoot his victim. But nothing happened and the gun he had bought for the purpose turned out to be a starting pistol. Was he so bad a soldier that he could not recognise what his weapon was? Perhaps at this stage he really was half-hearted in his purpose.

Bell then purchased a crossbow, saying he intended to catch Terry on a country walk, but somehow this plan did not work any more than the remote control bomb he planned to place under Terry's car. The problem here, he had explained to Roger Blackman, was that he was not sure where to get the explosives or a remote control detonator.

Then there was the 'car accident', Terry being run down by a hit and run driver. That failed because in the end Bell could not bring himself to do it when he saw Jean and Terry waiting at the prearranged spot. He did manage, however, in the guise of a visiting conservation officer looking after the welfare of local badgers, to provide Jean with a parcel of drugs with which to poison her husband. But the addition of powdered LSD and amphetamines to Terry's evening meal only made him violently sick and dizzy.

But Bell admitted that he was present at the house the night Terry went to the door and had his chest blown away. If he had deliberately fouled up his previous attempts on Terry's life, this time he really was prepared to carry out the plan. But, Bell said, his courage failed him. When it came to the point, he could not shoot a man in cold blood. It was Roger, standing beside him, who snatched the gun away from him and shot his stepfather.

On the strength of what Robert Bell told them, the police went to arrest Roger Blackman and his mother, the central figure in all this sordid affair. They arrived just in time to find that she had been rushed to hospital; she had taken an overdose. When she recovered, she was arrested and charged.

At the six-week trial which began at Hove Crown Court on 25th February 1993, Jean Daddow, Roger Blackman and Robert Bell were all charged with conspiracy to murder. In addition, Bell was charged with murder, the police not accepting his story that Roger Blackman had finally pulled the trigger.

Jean's emotional claims of innocence, her protestations of love for her husband, sounded hollow set against the accounts of how she had initiated all that occurred. The jury heard how over the months the former hairdresser had managed to divert much of the former banker's money into a network of thirty different bank and building society accounts, all under her control, and how, in the weeks before his death, she persuaded Terry to change his will, leaving her as the major beneficiary and cutting out his children from his former marriage. Though she hated her husband so much, Jean Daddow would not entertain the idea of divorce. It would have been too costly. She would have lost the greater part of the £300,000 she stood to gain from his death.

Not that Terry came out of the story very well. He was apparently talking about a money-making scheme, proposing to Jean that they spike the drinks of older women and then, while they were under the influence, they would photograph them in compromising positions. The opportunities for blackmail were endless.

There was a unanimous verdict of guilty in all three cases. For what Mr Justice Hidden said was 'as cold-blooded and callous' a crime as could be imagined, Robert Bell was gaoled for life with the recommendation that he should serve a minimum of 15 years and serve a concurrent 18 year sentence for conspiracy to murder. Roger Blackman and his mother were both gaoled for 18 years for conspiracy to murder. On hearing her sentence pronounced, Jean showed the same lack of remorse that had enabled her, as the grief-stricken widow, to weep for her husband on television.

At least before her arrest Jean Daddow did erect a headstone in memory of her late husband. It read, 'Terence Daddow – taken suddenly. In God's house but in my heart, your wife Jean'.

But the words chill.

HEY, BIG SPENDER

Soon after he arrived in Newick in 1983, Derry Mainwaring Knight was saying that his business was not doing well. Perhaps there was not too much call for a painter and decorator new to the village. People don't want their houses painted every year and when they do, they tend to stick to the firms they know. So, for the first few months, it must have been hard. But Knight persevered, tried to get to know people. He went round putting notices through letter boxes, not, as it happened, advertising his trade skills. No, he was inviting the villagers to prayer meetings in a local barn. But even they didn't take off. Nobody came. But it did bring Knight into closer contact with the rector, a good man, an earnest priest, with a strong congregation united in his favour. The Rev John Baker's thirteen years at Newick had been a resounding success.

But it was when the newcomer's wife, Gwendoline, had a serious car accident, that the rector really got to know Knight. He consoled him, counselled him, prayed with him, prayed deeply, fervently. So deeply, so fervently, that one night with the rector and his wife Alison sitting there with him, Derry slipped into a trance. That's when it all began, the whole curious business at Newick.

Seeing Knight slumped in his chair, John Baker knew at once what it was that had occurred. He was to say later, 'I recognised the state from having dealt with many people in similar states over the years as being due to demonic spirit infestation.' And then Knight began to speak. Or perhaps not Knight. 'The sound was coming out of his mouth,' the rector said, 'but not in his normal voice. As we were in prayer I said something like, "In the name of Jesus Christ I bind these spirits and adjure them to tell the truth and to declare their ground in this man's life."'

And the voice replied, 'You cannot have him. He belongs to Lucifer. He was dedicated by sacrifice as a child and he is a "Master of the Occult".' Only after further prayer and spiritual tussle could the rector dismiss the demon. And then, Knight recovered, prepared to tell his remarkable story to the rector of Newick.

His family, Derry Knight told Baker, had been involved in the black arts for thirty-three generations, a period of 850 years. At his birth he had been cursed by his maternal grandmother. And there had been a curious experience in his childhood. One night, he said, he had seen something standing at the foot of his bed. 'It was not human. It had the shape of a human being. But no facial features. I was told my life would be full of trouble. No good would ever come into my life and ultimately I would be utterly destroyed. I believe what I saw was an emissary from Satan. From that day on my troubles began.'

And yes, Knight confessed, he had done wrong. He had been evil. He had been dedicated to Lucifer by a defrocked cardinal in a sacrificial ceremony at the age of eight and was now in fact an archdeacon in a Satanic order which met in Hockley Woods in Essex. There, in the Satanic temple, wearing a gold headpiece and other ceremonial items, he conducted the mysterious rites of the order, going into a trance while the Devil spoke through him to his followers. When he was young, two platinum discs had been inserted in his head by a Satanic surgeon and this allowed him, he said, to be controlled from afar.

But for years now, he had thought about leaving the demonic sect and coming to Christ. It was not as if he did not understand about Christianity. Knight could cite the Bible, could interpret its meaning, much better than the usual churchgoer. This man, John Baker sensed, truly wanted to repent, wanted earnestly to leave the evil with which he had all his life been associated.

But it was not as easy as that. Knight was being groomed for the eventual leadership of his order. He was bound by his vows, his fears and his heavy debts. There was no way out for him, he told the rector.

But the man had to be saved, John Baker knew. The fight with Satan for this man's soul had to be won. From February 1984, for the next six months, Derry Knight lived at the rectory with the Bakers. He was given a room in the attic. 'Up there,' the rector said, 'he went into trances, ripped up Bibles in frenzy and spoke in demonic tongues. I became convinced he was so deeply involved that a straightforward exorcism would not have worked.'

But Knight knew what would work. And the rector agreed with him. If the Satanic regalia on which he had taken his vows and which had a powerful hold on him could all be obtained, and if they could then be destroyed, Satan's power over Knight would go.

It now seems an absurd tale, this business of getting hold of the regalia. Did such power really reside in chalices, robes, rings, sceptres? Both Knight and John Baker believed so. Those practising the black arts could use odd kinds of artefacts of control. No, the regalia must be purchased.

By March 1984 the deeply concerned John Baker had been in contact with some of his wealthy parishioners, people who sympathised with his own positive, charismatic approach to religion, pleading with them, persuading them, that here was a chance to save not just one man from the Devil but possibly two thousand other souls who were equally held in bondage to him. Would they out of the goodness of their hearts aid the deliverance of these misguided people? And they did. And in a succession of meetings over the following months they listened to Knight. They believed him implicitly.

Within weeks the rector had raised £24,925. By May he had found another £18,000. Then a further £12,500 flowed in. But more was needed, Knight said.

By October the rector had handed over £35,000 in used £50 notes. But there were further pleas in the next few weeks. By February 1985, Knight had received £98,000 and in May he was given another £25,000 to pay off more debts.

It was, of course, undeniable that, for a man with so many debts, a failed painter and decorator, he did live what some might have recognised as the high life. Because Derry Mainwaring Knight was a spender. He liked nice things, silk shirts, fancy jeans, purple suede boots, coyote skin jacket. He looked the part, 6 ft

Derry Knight (Daily Mirror)

tall, 20 stones, a big, overpowering sort of a man in his mid-forties. And then there were his cars, too. Range Rovers, Cadillacs, Lotuses. And a white Rolls Camargue, 'to match my image', needed in order to keep up sides with a rival for the leadership of the order. Once leader, all of the regalia would be his to destroy. He would strike a mighty blow against Satan.

Tens of thousands of pounds – always cash – go on jewellery, clothing and cars. And women, his mistress, his casuals, his prostitutes. They do well out of him. One has £900 for a blue fox fur and to another he gives £400 per week for sex. There is a Porsche for his mistress, Angela Murdoch. A young actress in rehearsal for panto is approached by Knight. Would she like a day out in Southend? She would and he spends £2,000 on her. Then she has three weeks in a rented bungalow. At a hotel in Forest Row there is a room set aside for after-dinner sex with another of his girls. One girlfriend is given a jeep and another a Lincoln Convertible. Then there is the riverboat 'bash', the £3,000 champagne party from Richmond to Shepperton, to which he invites disc jockeys Alan Freeman and David Hamilton.

Of course he had an interest in pop music. Newspapers were later to describe him as a record promoter. At one time he had claimed to have held managerial responsibilities with the groups Pink Floyd and Wham.

But oh, how the money flowed in.

And while all of this round of excess went on and on, the rector worked to encourage more and more giving. He was fortunate that he had access to so many deeply committed and extraordinarily wealthy Christians living locally. Only someone as wealthy as Lord Hampden of Glynde Place, who had already given £39,000, could have forked out for the Rolls. Only someone like the 'born again' Christian, Mrs Susan Sainsbury, wife of the MP for Hove, could pay out £80,000 over a few months. Michael Warren, the former High Sheriff, managed £36,000 and Gordon Scutt, a company director and officer of a Christian trust, found £25,000 for the rector. Other donors included Lord and Lady Brentford and Lord March. And of course there were others. Sincere, thinking Christians, they all seemed to have been possessed by a fervour which, some said, robbed them of all judgement. It was as though they felt themselves privileged to have received a direct message from God. They had to respond. Nor were they deterred by Knight who at one meeting told them, 'I don't have horns sticking out of my head.'

Not that there had not been some questions.

The Rt Reverend Eric Kemp, Bishop of Chichester, heard of the fund-raising in June 1984 and rang Baker to ascertain precisely what was happening in his parish. He was not totally convinced by what he heard and the following month appointed two clergymen to look into the matter further. They advised the rector to drop his support for Knight but he rejected their views.

In September, the rector reported to the bishop that further items, including a gold collar, a set of gold keys and a throne thought to be in the house of the head of the order off Pall Mall, needed to be purchased. 'I was told,' the bishop said later, speaking about the throne, 'that it was in a particular room in which it was surrounded by water and that Mr Knight would have to pay about £10,000 to enter the room.'

The bishop was concerned that at least there ought to be proof that the items were being acquired. After all, huge sums of money were being handed over and the donors were so trusting that they did not require any proof that the money was being properly used. Certainly, there ought to be some photographs of the purchased items. But Knight refused, the rector told the bishop. He did not want anything done that might alert the Satanists. These were dangerous people. If they were tricked or if any attempt were made to identify them, Knight's life, the rector's life, would be in real danger.

But regalia had been purchased, the rector said. He and Knight had smashed pieces up in the garden, had destroyed them and had then had the gold melted down. Every blow, he believed, was a blow against the Devil.

But why all this purchasing of regalia? Whilst the bishop acknowledged the real dangers of Satanism, he could not accept the enormous emphasis on the regalia. To become a Christian, in his view, Knight should repent and commit himself to Christ.

The bishop continued to monitor the situation and eventually, in March 1985, Knight was questioned by the police but he was not charged. In May, however, Knight was arrested and faced nineteen charges of obtaining more than £200,000 by deception.

At Maidstone Crown Court, in April 1986, the judge refused to deal with matters in secret. But lives were in danger, the rector said, if evidence about Devil worshipping objects was given in open court. There were, he said, 'things too dangerous to talk about' and he was to refer to the various articles of regalia simply as A, B and C. Nor in court would he reveal the name or any details of the Satanic organisation to which Knight claimed he belonged. It was too dangerous. Similarly, he had taken an oath on the Bible not to disclose details about the off-shore investment company, headed by a Satanist, into which £200,000 had been paid.

In the course of the trial, John Baker admitted that the man he had striven to save had surprised and alarmed him at times. For instance, he had at one point suggested they raise money by blackmailing a bank manager who had taken advantage of a woman client – Knight's mistress, as it turned out. The rector even had to persuade Knight not to use black masses against those he perceived as his enemies.

The rector told the court that he knew Knight consorted with prostitutes. He might even have known that he was running prostitutes at this time. Knight swore in fact that he was making £12,000 a week from his own business enterprise, sending his prostitutes to a clinic where their 'virginity' was restored by surgeons. But, Mr Baker said, he was not surprised by this. 'People who have a deep involvement in the occult don't normally get out in one nice, neat jump – the deliverance is a process,' he said.

And no, he was not the 'gullible fool' the prosecution suggested he was. He had been successful in the past in helping people to free themselves from the Devil.

There was no attempt on the part of the defence to say that Derry Knight was not a Satanist. No one tried to prove that he lived a purer than pure life. That he was depraved was not in dispute. But was he a conman? Or was he sincerely trying to escape the trammels of worshipping the Devil?

Certainly, Knight retained the support of several of the principal players in the drama. The rector never queried his sincerity. Susan Sainsbury, who had never met Knight but who had spoken to him on the telephone, continued to pray for him. She had sent him £80,000 but, 'as long as it was being applied to buying the regalia that was all right by me'. And she retained her faith in the rector. 'I believed all along what I was being told by Mr Baker,' she said. In her view, and that of the other donors, Satanism was more dangerous than most people thought.

Derry Mainwaring Knight was found guilty, sentenced to seven years' imprisonment and fined £5,000. It was revealed that he had served prison terms for embezzlement and rape. He had been dishonourably discharged from the Coldstream Guards. But none of this persuaded his most ardent supporters from praying for him and indeed believing in him as a man truly trying to escape from the Devil. He was convincing and highly knowledgeable. Nor did he deny his beliefs. In court he refused to take the oath on the Bible. He had taken an earlier oath on a sceptre which was, he said, 'of far greater importance than this court'.

So was Knight, as the prosecution claimed, 'cunning, devious and very close to being a pathological liar'? Was he a brilliant fraud? Or, as the defence would have it, was the prosecution case 'moonshine'?

Were the donors deluded? Well, if so, they remained remarkably steadfast in their support. They refused to believe that a significant number of items of regalia were sold on to other occultists. So was the Rev John Baker duped? Some say that he would not listen to advice, that it was arrogance and pride that made him believe he knew best. But then, very many of his parishioners continued to support him, praying for Knight on the first Sunday after he went to prison. It is interesting to learn too that Gwendoline Knight promised to stick by her husband.

Strange case. The debate continues.

Danger in Those Frilly Panties (Newspaper headline)

Colin told lies. Often. Whopping great lies that you would think nobody would believe. But they did and they were confused when they heard his stories and thought they were the truth. Sometimes people just didn't know where they were with Colin's lies.

And then one day, Colin decided he had had enough of it, this business of telling lies, and he decided to tell the the truth. And funnily enough, because you would think that everybody would be pleased that he had made up his mind not to tell any more lies, the people he thought were his friends turned on him and made him leave the country and cross the sea to another land.

And he did cross the sea to where he was no longer required to make up stories. No more headlines about frilly panties in the papers. No more saying that frilly panties caused friction and this in turn caused the premature detonation of bombs. No more putting the wind up people with headlines in the *News of the World* such as 'Emerald Isle Red Plot'. Three Trots, so the article said, had been smuggled from a Russian submarine off the coast of Donegal. Colin gave them that story along with a photograph of the submarine. No one but Colin seemed to know that the photograph had been taken off the Finnish coast. But now, for Colin Wallace, Liaison and Information Officer with Arun District Council, all that kind of work was over, no more disinformation any more, no more planting fanciful stories in newspapers. From now on, the stories were to be factually true.

There were different pressures now from the days when, as a high-flyer, marked out for rapid promotion, with the prospect of an MBE before him, he had been the youngest Army information officer in the Ministry of Defence with a rank equivalent to lieutenant colonel.

But Colin Wallace had come out of his native Ulster under something of a cloud. For he had, in the course of his security work there, become increasingly disenchanted with political machinations. He knew too much about bars and barns, back streets and high roads where the unexpected bombs exploded and rocket launchers were fired, where the death squads roamed, unaccountable to anyone; he knew too much about undercover work which led to innocent deaths; too much about the squalid cover-ups which protected child-abusers running children's homes in the Province, provided they served the cause; and too much about men in senior political and military positions in Ulster who were anxious to be rid of the current British government, led as it then was by Harold Wilson, a man they regarded as a Russian agent.

Propagandists and military spin doctors like Colin Wallace were at the bleak centre of this dark world in the 1970s. And in the end this 'psychological operation' was more than he could stomach. Not that Colin Wallace did not believe in the Ulster cause. He knew that the other side was just as ruthless and as totally unprincipled. But in his view, his own military and political masters were deeply dishonest. But then, the security world is never straightforward. Perhaps MI5 and MI6 who were deeply involved in Ulster affairs can only operate effectively if they are given a completely free hand. But when, after Wallace had formally reported to MI5 a leading Protestant paramilitary, a Bible-punching bigot, as being one of the main sexual abusers of children at the infamous Kincora Boys' Home, and the man continued to be protected, he became deeply disillusioned. He knew too that even the most salacious British newspapers had refused to run the story. And when he perceived the authorities to be ignoring the democratic principles at the foundation of their society, he had doubts about the morality of his own position. A campaign called Clockwork Orange, which had begun as an antiterrorist offensive, had turned into a campaign by security forces and certain of the military to smear the elected government.

It was Wallace's alleged offer of a restricted document to a journalist that was to lead to his dismissal from a service which he had served loyally but which, he now believed, was functioning in a wholly unacceptable fashion. And they got rid of him for doing what he had been expected to do for the past six years. And so, the tale-teller came to Arundel.

Colin Wallace was an outstanding success as a publicist for his new employers, the Arun District Council. He was able to use the outstanding organisational skills that he had honed in his service years. And when Arundel was selected to host the European finals of the TV game-show *It's a Knockout* in July 1980, the council could hardly have found a more competent man to make sure that everything clicked into place. Wallace threw himself into the organisation with the utmost enthusiasm arranging a day that would attract thousands to Arundel. Here they would see energetic teams of adults in colourful fancy dress climbing the walls of bouncy castles; crawling at speed through complex mazes of tunnels in red, green, yellow plastic; suspended over troughs of water while they jousted with inflatable poles; pushing giant balls through assault courses. The programme, broadcast from the Avisford Park Hotel, was one of the best and most ingenious ever featured on the popular series.

And Colin Wallace was more than instrumental in making the show a resounding success. He had had to travel to Lancashire and Switzerland to see other places making their preparations; he had had to meet representatives of TV and particularly the managers of *It's a Knockout*. There were long days crammed with journeys and meetings, urgent phone calls, unscrambling certain plans, revising others, so that all would be as ready as possible for the filming. And what a triumph it all was. Wallace might well have congratulated himself on having made a wise decision to come to Sussex, where he was so appreciated. His wife was secretary to the Duke of Norfolk and Colin was highly regarded.

And then the dark days began.

While they were working on the show Colin Wallace fell in love with his assistant, Jane Lewis. But she was married. In fact, she

Colin Wallace

had married Jonathan Lewis, a very highly regarded antiques dealer, only a year earlier and Wallace and his wife had been guests at the wedding. The affair blossomed as he and Jane worked together, sharing the excitement of the enterprise in which they were involved. They were rarely apart. And when Wallace went to Lancashire and Switzerland, Jane accompanied him. It was in these hectic weeks that their love grew. But their relationship never went beyond kissing and cuddling because Jane still deeply loved her husband Jonathan and for much of the time she felt guilty about what was happening.

On 5th August 1980, only days after the filming of the show, Wallace arranged a surprise dinner for Jane to thank her for her contribution to the successful event. It was held at the Avisford Park Hotel and was attended by friends and colleagues including the senior local policeman. He went to great lengths to keep the arrangements secret and perhaps when she arrived her pleasure was marred only by the fact that Jonathan had not turned up. But then she was accustomed to his having to make unexpected business calls, but it was disconcerting. She would have liked him to be there. But Wallace was there, giving her a framed photograph of herself in parachute gear. If Jonathan's absence spoiled the evening for her, so too did the sudden departure of Wallace, who claimed to be troubled by a recurrence of a stomach complaint he had suffered from earlier. He left the party, he said, to go home for his medicine.

It was later that night that the distraught Jane reported her husband missing. Some days later, two boys found his body in the river Arun. His distinctive orange Volvo was found in a car park in Arundel.

When he was first questioned by police, Wallace told them that he had last met Jonathan Lewis when they played squash together on 4th August. Then, after further questioning, he changed his story. He had in fact been telephoned by Lewis on 5th August, the day of the dinner party, and they arranged to meet at the swimming pool car park at 6.30 pm. Wallace admitted that Lewis had been concerned about his relationship with Jane. It needed to be discussed. They drove to Wallace's house in his car, leaving Lewis's Volvo in the car park. At the house they had a drink and discussed the situation. But Wallace told Lewis that the affair had ended, that he need not worry. Wallace intended to find work elsewhere. He was leaving the district. They had talked until 7.15 pm and their meeting had not in any way been acrimonious. Then Wallace dropped Lewis off at the car park and he had gone on to the dinner.

The police could not believe this story. It was too thin. Wallace was arrested and charged with murder. The accused man claimed that he had at first lied to police about the meeting with Lewis to spare Jane any embarrassment.

At his trial Daniel Hollis, QC for the Crown, observed: 'You could say it was the case of the man who never came to dinner and the case of the man who left a dinner party in order finally to dispose of his victim.' For Colin Wallace, it was alleged, had murdered Jonathan Lewis and had put his body in the boot of his car before the dinner. He had then, said the prosecution, absented himself from the dinner in order to dispose of the body.

The case against Wallace looked strong. There was a conceivable motive. The jealous and desperate lover is frequently a member of the cast in murder trials. And he had lied to the police.

The police said that when Wallace met the 29 year old Brighton antiques dealer, just before the surprise dinner party, he struck him, fracturing his skull. The body was put in the boot of the car lent to Colin for the television programme. Wallace had then gone to the dinner, where he told staff that Jonathan would be arriving later. He did not convey this information to Jane, who throughout the evening tried to contact her husband by telephone. It was then that Wallace had feigned illness and had temporarily left the party in order to dump the body in the river. But, according to medical evidence, although he had a fractured skull, Jonathan was still alive when he was thrown in the water, where he died from drowning.

At the trial Daniel Hollis for the prosecution said, 'The man you are trying was telling lies again and again and incorporated them in a written statement to the police. When he changes his story how do you know whether he is telling the truth or more lies?' This blow to Wallace's credibility was significant. But it was ironic that a man so well versed in the arts of deception should make such an ill-constructed case for himself.

His reason – 'I did not tell the truth because I believed I was the last person to see him alive' – failed to convince the jury.

And the whole calculating cold-bloodedness of the matter, how he had calmly gone on to the dinner, how he had engaged in the usual party small talk and then how he had so coolly excused himself and left to get rid of the young man's body, disgusted the jury members. Jonathan Lewis, lying unconscious in the boot of the car while his murderer ate dinner, was a powerful image.

There was of course other evidence too which told against the former soldier. A post-mortem on the body showed injuries 'clearly inflicted prior to death'. The Home Office pathologist, Dr Ian West, told the jury that Lewis had 'probably been hit by a karate blow' with the heel of the hand to the base of his nose while his head was held in arm lock. No weapon had been used. It was the sort of injury that an SAS man might have known how to deliver and, while it had been agreed by both prosecution and defence that no mention should be made of Wallace's previous career, his photograph in military uniform appeared in some national newspapers. Information of this kind can influence, as Colin Wallace knew all too well, and it could be surmised that he had been trained to deliver karate blows of this nature.

And there were other factors for the jury to consider as the witness statements were presented. What was Wallace doing looking in the boot of the TV company's car some days after Lewis's death? He said he was searching for a pen he had dropped under the spare wheel. And where was the missing rubber mat from the car? There were blood traces in the car. Had the mat been stained with the dead man's blood? Had Wallace thrown it away? Somebody else mentioned that Wallace had been asking about tides.

And Jane Lewis, in the witness box, who admitted the affair with Wallace, said that, when the police found her husband's car at Arundel and she also learned that a white Austin Princess, like the one Wallace had the use of, had been seen in the area, she became suspicious. She had asked Wallace, 'Is it anything to do with you?' But he had denied it.

As it happened, after legal submissions the murder charge was withdrawn by Mr Justice Kilner Brown. Instead, Wallace was charged with manslaughter. The judge did say, however, that it was beyond question that Jonathan Lewis died by drowning and that he was alive when he entered the water.

For the defence, blood found on the car matched that of three car assembly workers who had been preparing the vehicle at British Leyland's Cowley plant. During the course of the job, they had each cut their hands and this was where the defence claimed the blood came from.

The possibility was also voiced that a Mr Y of Brighton – his name was never made public in court – who was involved in smuggling stolen antiques out of the country, was responsible for Lewis's murder. Lewis, a reputable dealer, had even warned his wife about Mr Y's activities. Had he discovered dangerous information which was to lead him to his death? But such a suggestion was heard by the jury and presumably not proceeded with.

On 28th March 1981 Colin Wallace was found guilty and was jailed for ten years. Mr Justice Kilner Brown said it was a horrifying case and one of the worst he had tried.

Wallace was released from prison in 1986, still claiming to be innocent of any attack on Jonathan Lewis. He had been the victim of a plot, he said. He and his supporters, in particular the journalist Paul Foot and his counsel Michael Mansfield, maintained that the murder of Lewis by criminal antiques dealers in Brighton had served the purpose of those who wanted Wallace out of the way. He was still regarded as dangerous, still speaking of conspiracies against the government, still talking about cover-ups for corrupt intelligence men in Northern Ireland. The murder of Lewis was just the opportunity those who sought to silence him had been waiting for. Discrediting the opposition was what they were good at, the security services; Wallace himself knew all about that kind of work. In his time, he too had been adept at 'dirty tricks'.

By 1990 Wallace at least had the satisfaction of hearing the MOD accept that his dismissal from the Army for passing on restricted material had been unfair. For that, he received £30,000 compensation.

But his battle was not over, for he still claimed to have been totally innocent of any assault on Jonathan Lewis. In 1996 his conviction was finally quashed. One is still entitled to wonder whether Jonathan Lewis was murdered by Mr Y. And did MI5 then step in and make Colin Wallace, a man they still saw as dangerous, the convenient victim of an elaborate plot? Whatever the truth of it, the Lord Chief Justice, Lord Bingham, delivered a damning indictment, saying that if the case as it was now put before the court had been presented in February 1982, Wallace's request for leave to appeal against conviction would have been granted and a new trial ordered. According to his counsel, the case against Wallace was 'fundamentally flawed'.

Wallace had always claimed that the prosecution 'had been disgraceful and totally dishonest'. The police, he said, had suppressed evidence relating to Lewis's murder. 'For the past 16 years,' he said, 'Home Office ministers have told MPs there is no reason to doubt the original findings and now key parts of the evidence have been abandoned and other parts discredited by experts.'

Wallace's argument was that the report that Lewis was killed by a karate blow had been manufactured to establish a link with his (Wallace's) army background. Some pathologists had said that such a powerful blow would have damaged the nasal bones and caused bleeding, swelling and bruising but of this there had been no evidence. In any case, Wallace had always claimed that he was not trained in unarmed combat.

Furthermore, at the trial the Crown had said that there was a two-hour gap between Lewis being knocked unconscious and his being thrown in the river. But the report of pathologist Professor Keith Mant concluded that the interval was very much shorter and this was never revealed to the jury. This disposed of the idea that Wallace had left the party to get rid of the body. Also there was no proof that Lewis's injuries had been inflicted in Wallace's house nor that his body was ever in the boot of the Austin Princess.

If the jury had known of this, he would not have been found guilty. And they certainly would not have discounted the evidence of a prime witness – a riding instructor who worked part-time in her parents' pub and who claimed she had seen Jonathan Lewis in there with an unidentified man at the time when, according to the prosecution, he was supposed to be lying unconscious in the boot of Wallace's car.

Colin Wallace could not have been more unfortunate. All the factors seemed to point to him as the guilty man. He seemed to have motive and he had opportunity. It may be that there were those who saw this as an opportunity to put a nuisance out of the way, ignoring the long years of brilliant service by an outstanding and patriotic servant.

Not that Wallace had helped his own case when he was first interrogated by the police. He had lied unsuccessfully.

And once upon a time he had been so good at lying.

RELEASE

If for most of us birth is the great wonder, then death continues to be the greatest mystery. And yet for Philip Steff, a minister of the Spiritualist Church, there is little that is mystifying about it. What we call death he describes simply as a leave-taking from this world and from the physical body, the point from which the steps to a new phase of development are taken – by most souls. It is just a few who remain behind, uncomprehending, unaware that their temporary stay in this world has come to an end. These are the souls whom Philip releases. So far, in nearly twenty years, he has been involved in 170 'cases' of this nature.

Prior to Philip being summoned, however, people have sometimes been disturbed by extraordinary and occasionally frightening happenings in their own homes. In Brighton, for example, Maureen Long was worried by a series of inexplicable electrical faults. There seemed to be just no sense in what was happening. Maureen began to fear there might be a fire in her flat if things were not sorted out. And so she had called in various electrical engineers to have a look at the wiring; she had taken the alarm clock into a shop in Brighton to see what the trouble was. But whatever she did, things did not improve. So light bulbs blew and constantly knocked out the fuse box; electric plugs burnt out; electric wires were found fused together and the clock continued to turn itself off and on. Whatever it was, there seemed to be no rational explanation and this alarmed Maureen and her family.

Eventually Maureen began to think that there might be causes which she did not really dare to consider. Was there no natural explanation? No one among the experts she consulted could find one. Was there some supernatural cause? What could she do?

It was then that someone told Maureen of the Bath Psychic Club. Perhaps they might be able to advise her, and in March 1991 she got in contact with the group. Could they offer some help?

On 8th April, Philip Steff and two colleagues, Derek Goodson and Stuart Taylor, travelled to Brighton from the West Country. Philip Steff, who had already achieved some celebrity as a lecturer and broadcaster on matters psychic, had been regularly featured on TV and radio, in newspapers and magazines and was extremely experienced as a medium. Derek and Stuart, both psychic, were also accustomed to visiting sites where there had been disturbances.

The three men were uncertain what it was they were going to find when they arrived. At times they had dealt with evil spirits whom they had had to exorcise. On other occasions it had been necessary for them to release souls stuck in limbo between this world and the next. Perhaps this was what they were to be called upon to deal with this time. There was a whole range of possible disturbances in houses when the 'reluctant dead' drew attention to themselves. Sometimes they moved objects and at other times they made their presence felt by the sound of footsteps. And sometimes they interfered with the electrics in houses they had once occupied. It certainly seemed from what they had heard that a 'release' was required in Maureen Long's home.

On arrival and after having introduced themselves to Maureen and her son and daughter, Philip and his colleagues set about acquainting themselves with the two-storey house, which was divided into flats. They followed their customary routine, entering each room and standing still in each location to absorb the atmosphere and to tune in to the types of energies they found there. Both Derek and Stuart found that the bedroom normally occupied by Maureen was cold, not in a physical but rather in a psychic sense. Stuart became aware of a presence which followed him around the rooms but, not being clairvoyant, he could not see who it was. Derek also found that when he was near Stuart, he too felt the chilly aura of the presence. The tingling in his hands was confirmation to him that there was an unseen presence nearby. At this stage, neither man conveyed to Philip what he had experienced in order not to influence his psychic responses.

When it was his turn to investigate, Philip found the same bedroom to be the focus of the psychic activity. But it was in the kitchen that, with his heightened psychic awareness, he experienced a powerful tingling down the spine, an indicator of some kind of nearby presence. Here he 'saw' a white haired woman with haggard features. She seemed to be wearing a white gown of the kind worn in hospital operating theatres. Though evidently 'in occupation' of the flat, the woman was agitated and Philip felt that they needed to help her as soon as possible. He decided that the most appropriate room to work in was Maureen's bedroom, where all three had felt such active psychic vibrations. The three members of the Long family were invited to the sitting but chose to stay in another room.

Stuart and Derek have a distinct role to play when these psychic explorations take place. It is their function to provide extra psychic energies for Philip's spirit guides. It is these extra energies which enable Philip to see clairvoyantly the presence in order to persuade him or her to 'go to the light', to the rightful place, 'the spirit world'.

Now the bedroom door was closed on the three men. Philip opened with a prayer, asking his spirit guide to help with the work. Minutes passed and Philip's breathing became laboured and quicker as he went into a trance. It was in this altered state of consciousness that his guide, Otto, took over, addressing the haggard woman in his throaty voice.

It was a 'release', sure enough. The woman had died but had failed to recognise her condition. She had died in this very flat but was unaware of it. She had not taken the necessary steps of departure from her earthly life. She had to be gently persuaded of her situation, made to recognise that she no longer belonged here, that she needed to move on to the next stage of development.

Philip Steff

There was no need for her to fear, she was told. All she had to do was to understand that her spirit body, though similar to her earthly body, was of finer vibration, less heavy than her previous one. She must see that it was time to join her friends and family who had already passed on beyond. She had to recognise that Maureen Long and her family had the right to live their own lives here, that she must disturb them no longer. Not that these souls always wish to move on. Sometimes they are afraid to do so; others do not accept the situation in which they find themselves. They cannot believe themselves to be dead. In the Brighton flat there was an undoubted reluctance on the part of the woman, the ghost, to pass on. Eventually, however, she acknowledged her situation. And left.

After some minutes during which Philip and his two colleagues recovered from the exertions which their psychic activities had imposed on them, the Longs came into the bedroom. Yes, they all said, there was something indefinably different about the 'feel' of the room. Its atmosphere was, in their words, 'less heavy'.

Philip then described the woman whom he had clairvoyantly seen. Maureen signalled him to wait. She went out of the room and returned with an old newspaper.

After the Second World War an RAF pilot and his wife had occupied the flat. Sadly, he had been mentally disturbed and had one day jumped from the balcony to his death. Over the succeeding years, his widow, burdened with grief, had become an alcoholic. More than once, the Fire Brigade was called to the flat when fires had been accidentally started. The last time she was taken to hospital, where she died as a consequence of smoke inhalation. It was she who was unwilling to leave the place, unable until Philip Steff's mediation to recognise the fact of her own death. At last she was rescued. And Maureen Long's life was restored to normality.

There are many such instances of the dead refusing to move on. Some continue to occupy houses for years, often displacing objects to draw attention to their situation which they find beyond understanding. Persuading them to move on from their earthbound state, encouraging them to accept that they need to be released, is the work to which Philip Steff, Derek Goodson and Stuart Taylor have committed themselves.

LOVE NEST BY THE SEA

Such a prim and proper place, Eastbourne. Perhaps not so much so today but back in 1924 few would contest the idea that it was genteel. After all, it was a town, so it was said, 'built by gentlemen for gentlemen'. No place for the cheap and sordid here. Eastbourne was not Brighton or Southend or Blackpool. It had a reputation. It seems, therefore, hardly surprising that when Officer's House opened up to guided tours there was an outcry. Simply dreadful. Thank goodness it was far enough away from the town centre. It was out on that unattractive area of scrubland and beach between Eastbourne and Pevensey. And now they'd had the nerve, some tasteless people, to open up the former head coastguard's whitewashed bungalow to the public.

'And this is the garden,' the guide would say. 'Miss Kaye was very fond of it. She told him she was delighted with it.'

Not that she'd been there very long. She didn't get there till 12th April and three days later, well …

The guide would take them inside, all these gawping strangers, with their silly remarks and their sly jokes.

'And here,' he would drop his voice, 'here's where it all happened.' He'd wave his arm airily round the little sitting room. Then he'd point out the fireplace. 'The coal-scuttle was there,' he'd tell them. 'Hit her head on that, her lover tried to tell the police, but they weren't having any of it. Too light, too small, they said it was, to do that amount of damage. If she'd fallen against the scuttle, she'd not've been killed like he said she was. Axe or poker, more like.'

Then they'd all be looking at the fireplace. They'd read their papers. They knew what had happened, what had been said in the court at Lewes. There had been a storm raging that night when

Patrick Mahon

he'd put her head on the fire. And her hair had blazed and her eyes had suddenly opened wide and at that very instant the room was lit up starkly and there was the loudest crash of thunder you ever did hear and he'd been frightened, he said, and he'd run out of the room.

Perhaps he'd gone into the scullery, where he had still so much work to do. Or did go he into the bedroom where he'd left the trunk with parts of her body in it?

The guided tours which attracted so many to Officer's House did not last long. Public opposition proved too powerful. Nevertheless, for many years, until it was demolished in 1954, the four-bedroomed bungalow was still a reminder of Eastbourne's most gruesome murder.

Yet to look at him, Patrick Mahon was an extremely personable man. The 34 year old murderer of Emily Kaye was certainly handsome. He was a man of flair. He had style. He was always smartly dressed and many testified to his pleasant, open manner. He was charming and persuasive, this consummate and unrelenting womaniser. And he had a criminal record. When he was newly married and working in his native Liverpool, Mahon had been fired for forging a cheque from his workplace. He had used the money to take a lady-friend for a weekend on the Isle of Man. As it was a first offence he was bound over to be of good behaviour. And his wife Jessie forgave him.

Making a new start, they moved to Dorset but another theft from his new employers led to more trouble with the police. Again Jessie remained loyal to her errant husband.

Another move found them in Surrey. Here in 1916 he was caught breaking into a bank at Sunningdale. The housemaid of the bank manager, who lived over the premises, caught him in the act and Mahon hit her with a hammer. It is said that he was so overcome with guilt at what he had done that he remained with his victim until she came round. Before taking his leave, he had apologised and kissed her. Weeks later he was arrested and sentenced to five years.

Nothing seems to have altered Jessie's love for Mahon. She was waiting for him on his release and this time they set up house in Richmond. Jessie was working as accounts supervisor for a local company, Consols Automatic Aerators at Sunbury, and it was through her that Mahon gained employment with the same firm as a soda-fountain salesman. When the company went into receivership, Mahon, undeniably competent, was retained and promoted to sales manager. Then in the summer of 1923, Patrick Mahon met Emily Beilby Kaye, the receiver's secretary, a tall, outgoing 36 year old. Undoubtedly, Emily Kaye was attracted to Patrick Mahon and he was never able to pass up any opportunity to indulge his ruling passion.

They went out together and Mahon was to say later, 'As a result I realised she was a woman of the world, which knowledge came as rather a surprise to me.' Mahon the innocent.

Emily was deeply in love with him. There were meetings in restaurants. There were little outings. Perhaps there were occasional days away. There was certainly a flat in Soho to which they had access. If he was true to his character Mahon was still having brief affairs with other women. And Jessie, who knew him so well, doubtless had her suspicions but it was always difficult to pin anything on him.

There is a variety of theories about Mahon and why he murdered Emily Kaye. She was, when she died, several weeks pregnant and that was possibly a contributory factor. But it was certainly not the principal reason for her death.

Emily believed that Mahon was going to leave his wife and take her first to Paris and then to South Africa. She told her sister, Mrs Harrison, at Christmas 1923 that she had met a man she liked very much. In March Emily wrote to Mrs Harrison, telling her that she was engaged, that her fiance had secured 'a big post' in South Africa and that she would be going there with him. Mrs Harrison, excited at the prospect of a wedding for her sister, wrote back asking the man's name, asking what he was like and what were the wedding arrangements.

He was called, Emily said in reply, Pat Derrick Patterson and they were not intending to marry, she said, until after reaching South Africa.

But why had Emily called her lover by this name? Presumably because Mahon persuaded her that, in order to achieve a decent divorce settlement, he would not wish to advertise the fact that he already had a liaison with another woman. Or were there other reasons? Mahon's reasons?

Another of Emily's cousins, Major Beilby, a Hailsham veterinary surgeon, also had a letter. 'You will be glad and surprised to hear that I am engaged to a pal of mine. He has an appointment in Cape Town and I am going out with him in a fortnight's time. But I'm not going to get married right away. I shall get a post as secretary or something first to see what things are like. We are going in about a fortnight's time and this is probably a good-bye letter.'

Note again that Emily did not reveal her fiance's real name. Patrick Mahon certainly had a reason for concealing his identity and poor Emily Kaye never understood what that was.

Then there were her savings. At the end of 1923 Emily had £600 invested, a quite sizeable sum at the time. When she was murdered four months later she had only £71 in her account. Mahon's claim was that he knew nothing of her financial affairs. She had spoken to him about speculating in francs, saying there was a chance to make money and so, Mahon said, he had given her £125 as his share before Christmas 1923. But he left the dealing all to her. He said that he never asked her where she bought the francs nor how much she paid for them.

In February she had given him a £100 note. In early March, she had given him another £100 note. A third note was given to him a week or two later and this he cashed on 17th April. These windfalls, he asserted, were the results of her clever speculative investments.

Nevertheless, there were some odd circumstances. Why had he used false names when he cashed the £100 notes? Why had he endorsed them 'A. Lowe,' 'J. Edge of St Elmo, Staines' and 'J. B. Peters of 271 Hagley Road, Birmingham'?

The assumption is that he persuaded her to hand over the notes to him, that he was doing the speculating, that she was trusting him with her cash. The use of false names was to hinder any future investigation. When, incidentally, Mahon was asked for a reference from the agent, Mrs Muir, who let the bungalow to him, he had invented a referee named Douglas Horsfall at the Grosvenor Hotel in Birmingham. Constant subterfuges, endless

Police at Officer's House, Eastbourne

false trails, all designed to conceal the tracks of Mr Patrick Mahon of Richmond.

But Emily Kaye's money was running out. Now her lover had no further use for her. And if she disappeared from view, it would be assumed that she had gone to South Africa. Possibly at some time there might be a search for the non-existent Pat Derrick Patterson.

Mahon and Emily decided to spend some days away and he rented a bungalow on the Crumbles between Eastbourne and Pevensey – in the name of Waller. He later said that it was Emily's wish that they spend time together. She wanted to prove to him what a wonderful wife she would be. He insisted that the notion of his leaving his wife and going to South Africa was all her idea and he was not going to fall in with her plan. She was insistent, Mahon said. More likely, he persuaded Emily to go to the bungalow because that was where their story was to end.

They took occupation of Officer's House on 12th April. It was in the course of an argument in the bungalow some days later that

Emily was killed. In his statement to the police on 2nd May Mahon gave his account of what occurred.

On Wednesday, 16th April, Mahon claimed Emily had insisted that they go back to London. She intended to visit friends and told him he was to go to the passport office. But he had not gone to the passport office, he said. All the way back by train to Eastbourne they squabbled about this. Did he mean to marry her or not, Emily demanded. Did he really mean it when he said they were to go to South Africa? They needed passports if they were going to South Africa.

Back at Officer's House, the row continued. In his statement to the police Mahon described events as follows: 'We quarrelled over certain things and in a violent temper she threw an axe at me. It was a coal axe. It hit me a glancing blow. Then I saw red. We fought and struggled. She was a very big, strong girl. She appeared to be quite mad with anger and rage. During our struggle we overturned a chair, and her head fell on an iron coal-scuttle, and it appeared to stun her. This happened about twelve o'clock, midnight. I attempted to revive her but found I could not.'

Well, it's a not totally unbelievable scenario. Obviously not a murder. Case of manslaughter, that's what it sounded like. That's what Patrick Mahon made it sound like.

'The reaction after the struggle having set in, the consequences to me came home with stunning force. I put the body in the spare bedroom and covered it up with her fur coat.

'I came up to London on the morning of 17th April and returned to the bungalow fairly late, taking with me a knife which I had bought in a shop in Victoria Street. I also bought at the same shop a small saw.

'When I got back to the bungalow I was still so upset and worried that I could not then carry out my intention to decapitate the body. I did so on Good Friday. I severed the legs from the hips, the head, and left the arms on. I then put the various parts in a trunk in the bedroom and locked the door.

'I have been down several times since wondering how I could dispose of the body. On Saturday, 19th April, I stayed at the bungalow, also Sunday and came back to London on Monday. I did not touch the body either on Saturday, Sunday, or Monday.

'I again went to the bungalow on Tuesday and on that day I burnt the head in the sitting room grate and also the feet and legs.

'I came back to town late on Tuesday night or Wednesday morning, 23rd April. I went down again on Friday night, 25th April, and stayed at the Sussex or Clifton Hotel that night, going over to the bungalow about 10 o'clock on Saturday morning, 26th April.

'I had to cut up the trunk. I also cut off the arms. I burned portions of them. I then boiled some portions in a large pot in the bungalow, cut the portions up small, put them in the brown bag, and I threw them out of the train while travelling between Waterloo and Richmond. These portions were not wrapped up in anything. This was about 10 o'clock on Sunday night, 27th April. The bag to which I refer is the one now produced to me.

'I had intended to go home on Sunday night, but as I could not dispose of all of the portions between Waterloo and Richmond, I went on to Reading and stayed at the Station Hotel in the name of Rees. Next morning I came to London and left the bag in the cloakroom at Waterloo station. I had disposed of the remaining pieces between Waterloo and Reading on 27th April.

Were these the real facts of the case? Or had Mahon presented an ingenious defence?

Was it was all the panic of a desperate man who found himself in a terrifying situation? That is how Mahon presented the situation to the police officers at Scotland Yard, portraying himself as a man quite bewildered by what had befallen him. Just because of a silly argument with a lady-friend and a struggle which had ended in her death. And panic had gripped him, driving him on to complete a hideous task.

Yet it was ironic how Patrick Mahon was found out. It was the ever-loyal Jessie who unintentionally brought the affair out into the open. She was never surprised by the irregularities in her husband's life. She was accustomed to his absences but recently he had been away more frequently than usual. And an acquaintance had told her that Patrick had been seen at Plumpton races on the Easter week-end. Was he, she wondered, starting his gambling again? Looking for clues as to what he might be up to she turned

Emily Kaye

out the pockets of one of his suits. All she found was a railway left-luggage ticket. She had a friend, a former railway policeman. She wondered if he could help her. Could he go to Waterloo and pick up the piece of luggage? Perhaps he could just look inside for her. Perhaps he'd find something which explained what Patrick was up to.

When the Gladstone bag was opened it explained all too well what it was that Patrick Mahon had been up to. For the bag contained a torn pair of knickers, two pieces of silk, a cook's knife and a brown canvas tennis bag marked EBK. Everything was heavily bloodstained. And everything smelt strongly of disinfectant.

Jessie's friend replaced the bag in left-luggage and called the police. Mahon was arrested when he turned up to collect the bag. Eventually he gave his account of what had occurred.

When the police went to Officer's House, they found the trunk with Emily's remains in four parcels in the bedroom, ashes in the fire grates in the dining room and the sitting room, and saucepans in the scullery with boiled liquids and fats.

Perhaps as he spoke to the police Patrick Mahon thought they might accept his version of what had occurred. Perhaps they would think everything happened the way he said it did. There had been a row, a struggle, a fatal accident. And then, in a panic, he had tried in this gruesome fashion to be rid of the body.

Certainly that was Mahon's defence at Lewes when his trial for murder opened on 15th July 1924. He made an impression in his smart tailored suit. And how could he not make an impression with his handsome features, tanned artificially so it is said with tobacco juice? Style, flair, panache. You had to believe him. A man as handsome as he was couldn't possibly have done what he was being accused of.

Despite his defence, there were certain telling factors against Mahon. He had made mistakes. For example, he was asked why he had bought a special knife for the dismemberment. Because Emily had used the one in the kitchen for their meals, he said. Somehow it did not seem right to use it on her. But had he not said in his statement to the police that he had purchased the ten-inch knife on 17th April? But he had bought the knife and a small meat saw at the Staines Kitchen Equipment Company in Victoria on 12th April, the day he went down to Officer's House with Emily. Proof that he intended to kill her and dismember the body.

As for Mahon's assertion that Emily had died after hitting her head on the coal scuttle, that was dismissed by Sir Bernard Spilsbury who had conducted the post mortem outside in the garden at Officer's House as the stench of death had been so foul. Such a flimsy item, the pathologist stated, could never have caused anyone's death.

There are other factors which confirm that Patrick Mahon was not simply a womaniser who had bad luck when he had a row with Emily Kaye. There was more to it than that. He was a truly callous man.

Emily went down to Eastbourne in advance on 7th April, excited at the prospect of moving into Officer's House with Mahon. Up in Richmond, however, Mahon had by 10th April met 32 year old Ethel Duncan. Late one rainy evening, she had been going home and the gallant Mahon was there to speak to her and like a true gentleman to escort her home. On the way, he chatted with his usual charm. His name, by the way, was Pat, he told her. Would she like to go out to dinner with him one evening? Of course she would.

On Tuesday, 15th April, Mahon sent Ethel a telegram arranging a meeting at Charing Cross the next day. The following day, when Mahon met Ethel Duncan at Charing Cross, Emily Kaye was dead. And though he knew what the situation was back at Officer's House, Mahon invited her there for the Easter weekend.

On Good Friday morning Mahon cut off Emily's head as he could not otherwise fit her body in the trunk. Then he went off to meet Ethel Duncan at Eastbourne station. After lunch they took a taxi ride round the countryside, and then had dinner in Eastbourne before returning to the bungalow. Ethel detected that another woman had been there. There were cosmetics and a pair of shoes. His wife's, Mahon explained. And there was the bedroom she must not go in, quite like the forbidden room in the Bluebeard story. Ethel glimpsed a trunk inside. It contained, Mahon said, extremely valuable books belonging to a friend.

On the Saturday afternoon, while Ethel went shopping in Eastbourne, Mahon went off to Plumpton races. On the way there he sent a telegram to himself at the bungalow. In the evening he picked up Ethel. The telegram was waiting when they arrived back at Officer's House. It was an urgent message from someone called Lee. Mahon must return to London on the Monday. Thus he was rid of Ethel, who had served to take his mind off matters for a day or two. Now he had to get on ridding himself of the remains still in the trunk. At the end of the week he deposited the bloodstained Gladstone bag in Waterloo station and Jessie was beginning to worry more and more about what he was getting up to. In a day or so, she would look in his suit pockets.

Perhaps he was unlucky. If Jessie had not been so curious about her husband's whereabouts, Mahon would never have been caught. There was no head. After burning it, he threw the ashes away. He would not have been traced as the man who had leased Officer's House. That was someone called Waller. And, incidentally, no murder weapon was ever found. The view of the police was that Emily Kaye had been beaten on the head with the axe that he said she had thrown at him. Possibly there had been no row between them; possibly he struck the unsuspecting woman one massive blow from behind, in the sitting room.

Patrick Mahon, the cold-hearted charmer, was sentenced to death and hanged at Wandsworth Prison on 3rd September, 1924.

IF YOU GO DOWN TO THE WOODS TODAY

There are places which earn unenviable reputations. Perhaps they deserve them; perhaps they do not. But stories sometimes attach to the most unlikely locations. Take Clapham, for instance, just north of Worthing, and its wood. In the 1970s and 1980s it was said that the birds no longer sang in the wood, that the wildlife had gone; there was talk of mysterious fires and UFOs. People spoke of the eeriness of certain parts of the woodland, the sense of some unseen presence. They talked of their uncertainties when the winter light began to fade, when summer breezes so suddenly shook the boughs. Some spoke of their feelings of anxiety, illness and even of an actual physical force that seemed to pull and tug at them.

And then there were the people who went missing …

On Friday 2nd June 1972 Police Constable Peter Goldsmith failed to return to his Steyning home from work and his wife reported him missing. When he did not arrive for the next morning's shift a huge search was instituted. The 6ft 6ins former commando was not an easy man to mistake. He was seen in the mid-afternoon of 2nd June, carrying a brown canvas holdall, walking in the direction of the Downs above Steyning. Huge numbers of police, some with dogs, some on horseback, scoured the Downs. Helicopters surveyed the area. But there was no success even though the hunt continued throughout the summer. On 22nd September the police admitted that their intensive searches had been unsuccessful.

Every possibility had been considered. Had the missing man any work worries? His wife thought that he was concerned about the career of a nephew, another policeman, who had been temporarily suspended. But on the day of his disappearance, she said her husband was perfectly normal. When he left the house he had told her he was going to the bank.

On 13th December a farmer from Fulking, Edward Harris, out shooting, found Goldsmith's body at Pepperscoombe in Clapham Wood, an area that had been thoroughly searched. But the body lay in dense bramble and was now covered with leaves. Perhaps that was why it had been missed. The growth was impenetrable and the policeman's remains, considerably decomposed, had to be cut out from where they had lain. Next to the body was a bottle which contained an unidentifiable brown liquid. Whatever that mysterious liquid was, it was not poisonous. Nor had Goldsmith taken any other poison. Nor had he suffered a heart attack. And he was in good health. Indeed, the cause of the policeman's death was a complete mystery to the medical men.

The West Sussex Coroner, Francis Haddock, said that certain aspects of the case suggested suicide, but the family vehemently denied this possibility. In the event an open verdict was reached.

Had this puzzling occurrence anything to do with a matter which for some time had apparently been causing Goldsmith some anxiety? Some months earlier, in April 1972, the body of a young woman had been found on the Downs. According to witnesses, Goldsmith was deeply affected by this particular death. As a Coroner's Officer, he had attended many inquests and it might have been expected that he would be hardened to sudden and unpleasant deaths. Not so. One day when they were burning old documents relating to inquests, Goldsmith said to a colleague, John Grigson, 'All these suicides and sudden deaths come back to me and make me feel sick.' What seems to have most perturbed Goldsmith was the open verdict in this particular case. It dissatisfied him. There was more to it, according to Goldsmith, than had ever come out. There were suggestions that he had uncovered some details, unspecified, and that he was at the time of his disappearance investigating the matter unofficially. Did he think it was a murder? Had he stumbled onto something which explained the woman's death and had he suffered for it?

And what about the location in which Goldsmith's body was found, only half a mile or so from where the woman's body had been found? It lay undetected deep in a bramble patch. One of the forensic experts dismissed the idea that the body could have been placed there by others. But could the constable really have made his way through to such a scarcely accessible spot alone and voluntarily? And if he had waded through the entanglement, would this not have ripped his clothing and his flesh?

And there are a couple of other small mysteries to add to the plot. What happened to the holdall that he was carrying when he was last seen? And what of the other strange factor? The autopsy showed that he had not eaten or drunk for several days before death. So where was the constable between the time he disappeared and the time he died?

In July 1975 Leon Foster, a fit 66 year old, a regular Downland walker, went missing and his body was not recovered for three weeks. It was impossible to tell from the advanced state of decomposition the cause of death. The Coroner's court brought in an open verdict, but suggested that most probably Foster had been overcome by the summer heat and had simply lain down to die in the wood. There was in the body a small amount of alcohol but, interestingly again, Leon Foster had not eaten or drunk anything for some days before his death. Odd? And why was there what appeared to be a makeshift bed of straw beside the body?

Then on 31st October 1978 the former vicar of Clapham and Patching, the 65 year old Rev Harry Neil Snelling, disappeared. He had that morning kept an appointment with his dentist in Goring. He took the bus back to Findon and according to witnesses was in good heart for he spoke to several people during the journey. At Findon he rang his wife at Steyning, as they had arranged that she would pick him up in their car. Unfortunately, she told him, the car was out of action. He would walk back, he told her. He was undeterred by the prospect of a five mile walk. The Rev Snelling was last seen passing Findon Park House, just preparatory to climbing the steady rise to the Downs. When he failed to come home, his wife called the police.

The following day the route that he had clearly intended to follow was searched by a team of twenty-five police officers but there was not the slightest clue as to where the Rev Snelling had gone. The search went on through the night and over the next several days. As usual tracker dogs and light aircraft were used, but without success. Naturally, people speculated. He was a shade doddery, said some of those who knew him. Others thought that he might have committed suicide. He had a history of depression and years earlier, before he came to Clapham in 1960, he had attempted suicide. But even so, that could scarcely explain the missing body. And that body was missing for nearly three years.

In August 1981 Michael Raine, a Canadian walking the Downs, came across a corpse in the Wiston Barn area. Being in a hurry to catch a flight, Raine wrote to the Sussex police, describing his find and enclosing a rough map of where the body lay. It was found 150 yards from the north edge of Clapham Wood near a MOD restricted zone. This part of the wood, though less frequented than other areas, had been searched previously. The body was Snelling's, identified by a ring and a wallet, as well as by inspection of dental and medical records. It was not possible to say what was the cause of death. Again an open verdict was returned. Was this a suicide? Ironic if it were, for the Rev Snelling had established a branch of the Samaritans in Steyning.

On 28th September 1981 Jillian Matthews, a divorcee in her late thirties, disappeared from her home in Worthing. Everything pointed to her having just popped out to go shopping in the town. Not unnaturally, her friends were worried even though she had gone missing on other occasions. But then she had always contacted them by telephone. This time there were no phone calls. Had she had a mental breakdown, they wondered. She had been receiving treatment for schizophrenia but was understood to be on the way to recovery. Her friends had been fully confident that she was much improved in recent months.

Some weeks later, on 14th November, her body was discovered in the wood by members of a shooting party, about 60 yards from Spithandle Lane in Wiston, five miles or so from Steyning. Strange though that only a fortnight earlier the area had been shot over and there had been no sign of the corpse. What the forensic team were able to establish, although her body was badly decomposed, was that Mrs Matthews had been raped and strangled. Her pants and tights were missing. Her killer has never been found.

How was it that a woman on her way to the shops should end up miles away in Clapham Wood?

The investigation into the murder of Jillian Matthews was difficult. The police themselves issued a statement admitting they were having problems because a number of people in the Steyning area were 'reluctant to talk directly to police'. They set up a confidential telephone line and sent forty officers on house-to-house enquiries but no helpful information was forthcoming.

Some odd questions seemed to be coming out of all of this. How is it that four bodies have been found in more or less the same area? One was undeniably murdered. And the others? And what about the time-lag between the disappearance of the bodies and their discovery. Strange when thorough searches of the ground did not at first produce any results. And the state of decomposition was, in three of the cases, if not in the case of the Rev Snelling, who had been missing for nearly three years, unusually pronounced. And what about the fact Goldsmith and Foster appeared not to have eaten for days before their deaths? Had they been spirited away somewhere? Had they endured some kind of brief imprisonment?

Two researchers into these most curious matters have come up with quite alarming conclusions. Both of them are convinced that in the 1970s a coven of witches operated in the district. They are both of the view that the disappearances were related to their activities.

In the latter part of that decade Charles Walker of Worthing, a writer and researcher into the occult, was interested in what he kept hearing and reading in the local press about Clapham Wood. There were so many odd incidents. Three dogs had gone missing in the vicinity. There were reports of excessive 'cold spots' in the copse known as the Chestnuts. Some locals remarked that the woodland was no longer what it was. Where had all the nightingales gone, where were the foxes, the badgers, the rabbits which once were so prolific? It was as if the very life was being drained out of the place. Walkers in the wood spoke of sudden feelings of anxiety, unaccountable cramps. Two serious researchers confronted by a strange light took a photograph which, when developed appeared to show a goat's head, that old symbol of Satanism, of powerful evil? Or was it UFO activity? So many things were being suggested. And Walker felt that he ought to find out the truth. One way was to write to the local press. He wrote several letters. Did anyone have any ideas? Any information? Had anyone had unaccountable experiences in the neighbourhood of Clapham Wood? But there was nothing in the way of a useful response, until Walker's telephone rang early one November evening in 1978. The caller was male, his voice refined and educated. And he proposed a meeting. He had information. Could Walker meet him? This evening. Within half an hour. In Clapham Wood. Where the bridle-paths crossed. And he must come alone.

It cannot have been easy to enter that dark wood with all of its associations. Why in the wood? Why not call at his home? Why not talk on the phone? Why not meet in a cosy pub? Why go into the depths of that winter woodland, into the dark?

Plucking up his courage, Walker went to the meeting place. No one there. Not a sound save for the whisperings of the bare branches, the rustling in the shadowy undergrowth, sharp scampering sounds, the choked-off shriek of some small woodland creature. But no one came. Practical joke?

And then he heard a voice – he recognised it as his caller's – he was not to move, not to turn to look for the speaker.

Nor was he to ask questions. He was to listen.

The speaker was an initiate of the Friends of Hecate, that dread goddess. Did Walker wonder, even as the voice talked, about the goddess of suicides and sudden death? Had those found in the wood committed suicide? Or had something else happened to them? Was the speaker really a follower of the goddess of the hidden moon, the goddess of darkness when the grimmest deeds are carried out, the goddess of the crossroads where the most awful evil magic is practised?

It was here they met, the coven, Walker was told by his informant, whispering from the shadows. They came here each month. And there was always a sacrifice. Often, it was a dog. Walker doubtless recalled the dogs that had gone missing in the wood. And perhaps he remembered that the devotees of the goddess had in ancient Rome sacrificed dogs.

It was here at these woodland crossroads – remember crossroads where suicides and murderers were buried in distant times? – that the members of the coven gathered, Walker was told, although in wet weather they met in a barn. They had been coming here for the past ten years, but in another ten years or so they would move on to some other place from where 'to spread the word'.

Now, Walker had to take heed. There were people in high places involved, he was told, people who held positions of power and who would tolerate no interference. They would stop at nothing to ensure the safety of the cult. He had been warned.

Walker was then asked to leave the wood and not to look behind, precisely in the way that two or even three thousand years earlier, the followers of Hecate had left her sacred ground, warned not to to look back as they went.

As he walked away, did Charles Walker wonder about Hallowe'en, just a few days earlier? The old vicar, the Rev Harry Snelling, had gone missing in these woods.

Walker's experience in Clapham Wood was unnerving enough, yet he was not deterred from continuing his investigations. Shortly after the woodland encounter, he was cycling home, when he was knocked down by a hit-and-run driver. He was convinced that he was being warned rather more seriously. But even that did not deter him.

In the spring of 1979 Walker returned to Clapham village. In the grounds of the deserted manor house, said to be the oldest building in Clapham, he saw a medieval barn. Was this, he wondered, where the cult members met in bad weather? He went inside. Searching behind bales of straw, he saw covering the west wall a huge, brilliant painting, depicting the Devil and assorted demons. Hastily, he took photographs of it.

Leaving the barn Walker encountered a man with a shotgun, who followed him as far as the church. Of course, it might well

The huge wall painting of the Devil, found in a Clapham barn

have been a farmer, outraged at someone trespassing on his private land. But the threats he uttered did seem seriously intended.

Walker and Toyne Newton, another occult researcher, with whom he had teamed up, carefully studied the photograph of the painting in the barn. They had no doubt that it represented the old goddess Hecate.

Later the two researchers had further information from an anonymous letter writer. They were told that the cult was controlled by a doctor and two women, one of them young, the other middle-aged. They did not attend every meeting but when they did there were human sacrifices. Walker and Newton inevitably wondered if there could be some connection with the people who had disappeared, Goldsmith, Foster, Snelling ... as yet, Jillian Mattews had not been murdered. Their informant told them that the cult rented land in the area on the pretext of pheasant shooting. From Walker's account and that of Newton, other people visiting the woods at about this time frequently met men with shotguns barring their way. Gamekeepers perhaps? Or perhaps men out shooting? Or perhaps ...? When Newton visited the village and woods with a photographer they encountered some hostility from locals.

When researching his book *The Demonic Connection*, Toyne Newton says he could sense the very malevolence which hung heavily about this area. 'It was as if the very air and atmosphere itself had been charged with thousands of tiny throbbing electrons emitting a very subtle but strong vibration, like walking into charged-up cobwebs. You want to brush them away but you can't.'

Postscript: Unfruitful conversations with the author – winter 2000–2001

He is reluctant to say anything really, the first one. Doesn't want to talk about it at all. 'Just an old story. Nothing in it,' he says, conveying the idea that whoever suggests otherwise is a gullible fool. There's a complete barrier that cannot be breached. He is not going to concede anything. 'Just one of those things,' he says. 'Dogs do go missing.' The people? 'Forget it. Just an old story, a fuss about nothing. Overheated imaginations.'

Another one is equally hesitant. He, however, doesn't dismiss things out of hand. He says, 'Well ...' and 'Could be ...' and expels deep breaths before he answers. Not that he is saying he believes those tales. 'It's all a long time ago,' he says, as if that renders all speculation pointless.

And a lady, she says, 'I don't think all those stories should be brought up again. It wasn't very nice, you know, the police asking questions and those other men, those investigators, the ones who wrote the books, they didn't help this village.'

But, remember, if you go down to the woods today ...

OBSESSION

Big boy, Olly, real name Clive Olive. But in fact he already had several aliases. Six feet tall, well built. A hard nut, you could see at a glance, even if he was only sixteen. Didn't take much to work out, from the shoulder length hair, the torn denim jacket and trousers and the motorcycle boots that he was a Hell's Angel. Or almost. He was not quite an Angel, not an authentic one anyway, because he had no motorcycle, though he was talking about getting one when he'd saved up enough money. So he had to be content to belong to a kind of lower breed of Angel, the kind of group that the true Angels despised, one of the Angels' poor relations. He was one of the Angels who went on foot.

For a time, Olly had belonged to the Sussex Mad Dogs and that was cachet enough. Tell anybody you belonged to the Mad Dogs and you earned a bit of respect because they were well known around Brighton and Worthing. Known for their steel toecaps, known for using them too. A violent mob, the Mad Dogs. That was their creed, violence, and nobody was safe from them. And when he left and joined the Cougars in Hove they had taken it pretty badly. In fact, they'd beaten him up really savagely. Nobody left the Mad Dogs. And they'd taken his colours from him, the colours which proclaimed who they were, the insignia on the back of their jackets. So, in effect, they were telling him that he hadn't left them: they were throwing him out.

Still as a Cougar he felt entitled to swagger. And fight. Some nights he'd be down in Brighton and he'd take on anybody. Hard man. Sixteen years old.

And he knew about drugs. Knew where to get them. So when Gerry from Coventry rang him, when Gerry told him over the phone that he had certain needs, Olly agreed to meet him.

It was on the night of 27th February 1973 that they first met. Olly had just finished at the Gondola restaurant where he did a spot of washing up and he went out and there was Gerry from Coventry and another couple, a man and a woman, in the van. And they motored round and round that night. But they didn't come across any drugs. Poor night really. But they agreed to have another go the next night.

And so, the following night, Olly turns up again and there's the 12 cwt Austin van again and Gerry and the man and woman. They'll have another go, try to be more successful tonight. So Olly climbs in the van, settles himself down.

And that was the last time anybody ever saw him alive.

On 19th April a fully clothed body surfaced in Aldrington Basin at Shoreham. It was brought to the surface by turbulence from a ship's propeller. But this corpse hadn't just fallen in the water. Round his shins and ankles there were several loops of rope and at the end of the rope was a plastic bag containing stone blocks. It was Clive Olive all right. Seven weeks earlier he'd been reported missing by his mother and here he was. No doubt about it. In his pocket there was a white metal bracelet, 'Olly' inscribed on the face and on the reverse 'Julie'. And there were the tattoos: a heart and HAC – Hell's Angels Cougars.

But what was remarkable, what chilled the blood, was the pathologist's report. There was no sign of any head injuries, no fractured skull, no indication of strangulation. It was Professor Hugh Johnson's professional opinion that Olly had been alive when he entered the water. Perhaps he had even been conscious.

The police operation to discover the murderers of Clive Olive immediately focused on the Hell's Angels. And it was a very difficult enquiry. The world of the men and boys known as Wank and Randy, Simple and Loner, Gyppo, Tramp, Bluey, Felix and Zombie had its own codes which were often inaccessible to the police. As the Annual Police Report of 1973 indicates: 'It was necessary for the officers involved to virtually learn a different language, or rather jargon, in order to understand what people being interviewed meant. The enquiry revealed a very unsavoury sub-stratum of our modern society, its devotees owing allegiance only to their own small groups and with a complete disregard for what has come to be recognised as civilised behaviour.'

In other words the police faced a wall of silence and hostility. The tribes clammed up. They were surly, aggressive, unhelpful. They displayed a profound indifference to the fact that a boy, one of their own, had been done to death in a particularly cruel manner. Perhaps they regarded what had occurred as an internal matter.

Nevertheless, there were the odd whispers. Apparently, somebody had been looking for Olly, somebody who meant to get even with him. Within twelve days of finding the body, police made three arrests. They took into custody Brian Moore, a 21 year old scaffolder, his 18 year old sister, Christine Dorn, and her husband, Albert Dorn, a builder's labourer aged 27, all living at that time in Pankhurst Avenue in Brighton. They were charged with the murder of Clive Olive between 27th February and 1st April 1973. All were former members of the Mad Dogs. All still carried the attitudes of their old gang. Moore was sometimes known as 'Angus', Dorn as 'Little Al' or 'Mouse' and Christine as 'Butch'.

The confession didn't take long in coming from Moore. He'd sat across the desk from Detective Sergeant Colin Taylor and at first he'd been outraged, had refuted every suggestion that he knew about the murder, even denied having heard of Clive Olive. He'd just sat there, confident, scornful, his long red hair tied back, looking like a pirate. Knew nothing, he said.

But then, he'd seized hold of the detective's hand. Suddenly, there was a change. 'Please, please,' he said, 'you've got to help me now.' There was a girl and he didn't want her involved. He'd tell Taylor about it just to keep her in the clear.

And so he began to tell his story.

It was about the girl really. That was what it was all about. He'd met this girl, Paula Merritt, earlier in the year and he'd fallen in love with her. Seriously. She was a grammar school girl and really intelligent and nice. She'd changed his habits. He was different now, completely altered. He didn't do drugs any more. He loved her more than anything or anybody. He respected her. She was different. 'She was not one of these old slags,' he told the detective. She was a really decent girl and one he wanted to settle down with. She was neither a Hell's Angel nor a drug taker.

'Still got your white wings?' Moore had asked her. She did not know what he meant. He explained, asking her if she had ever had sexual intercourse. She'd told him about Olly, about how she used to go out with him. And she told him that Olly had raped her on her sixteenth birthday in September 1972.

She'd gone with Olly to his mother's flat in Norfolk Terrace in Hove but his mother was out. Olly had gone into his bedroom. It was a bit of a mess, he said, and would she like to give him a hand to clear it up. Then, when she went in, he had put his arm around her and had raped her. She had put up a struggle but Olly was too strong. After the rape Paula had not wanted to see him again. Certainly she never went out with him any more.

And that was when it had all gone sour. Moore had taken it badly. He had been incensed. And then, towards the year's end he began to hear stories. Olly had begun boasting about having sex with Paula. It was too much for Moore. He couldn't stand this. It had to be stopped but where was this Olly? He couldn't get him out of his mind. He spoke of it constantly to Paula. He didn't know Olly but he would find him and beat him. Other times, he even said he would kill him. It had become an obsession, so much so that it interfered with their own love making. 'I didn't like to make love to Paula in the normal way,' Moore said, 'because this was the position in which she was raped.'

There was one day when Moore insisted on a re-enactment of the rape but they did not go as far as intercourse because they both broke down in tears. Then another time, they held a cleansing ceremony when they conducted a ritual burning of the clothes Paula wore the night she was raped, together with Moore's Hell's Angels' clothing.

He would find him, Moore told her. He'd look out for Olly, somebody would know him. Moore spent £30 or more seeking information about Olly's whereabouts. And finally someone told him that he worked in a restaurant called the Gondola.

Perhaps Olly had word now that someone was on the look-out for him. He seemed to be cautious in the last few days of his life. Even so, when 'Gerry from Coventry' telephoned him, asking him if he could lay his hands on drugs, Olly agreed to meet him.

Clive Olive, known to his friends as Olly

On the first night they drove round and round in the van, the four of them. But Olly couldn't find them any drugs. 'No matter' Gerry from Coventry told him. 'See you tomorrow night.'

And the van picked him up the next night and drove along the seafront towards Shoreham.

It was when he was in the van, its interior painted a crude pink, that the truth dawned. Moore started asking him about Paula. Couldn't remember her, Olly said. He had lots of girls. Couldn't remember every girl.

Now under arrest and speaking to Detective Sergeant Taylor, Moore told him: 'I said: "The one you raped, you bastard," but he denied knowing her.'

Perhaps it was then that Olly realised he wasn't with Gerry from Coventry. And it must have struck him that the three of them in the van weren't after drugs. The night before they had been looking for a quiet place where Moore could beat him up but there had been too many police cars about. But tonight was different.

Moore had taken a truncheon out and threatened Olly, and it was then that he admitted it. Yes, he said, he had hurt her. 'He said it all cocky like,' Moore told the detective.

At that point Moore, on his own admission, went berserk. Dorn was driving, Christine at his side, and in the back Moore released his rage on the terrified Clive Olive. In his statement to Detective Sergeant Taylor, he said 'I belted him with my fists once. He started crying and there was a lot of swearing. I knocked him back with my hand and called him a bastard. Straight afterwards I belted him with the stick a couple of times. I don't remember how many times. He gave an almighty scream.'

Dorn was becoming anxious now, fearing that things were going too far. Both he and Christine had thought Moore was going to give Olly a good hiding. They both believed that he deserved that. But there was a silence when, after a ferocious crack on the head with the truncheon, the boy slumped in his seat. Looking over his shoulder and fearing the worst, Dorn said, 'You have killed him.'

Moore said, 'I lifted his head with my truncheon and his eyes were all staring. It was diabolical. I thought he was dead.'

They drove around Shoreham for a while wondering what they ought to do now, Dorn and Christine in particular terrified at the way things had turned out. Dorn wanted to drive Olive to hospital and leave him there in case there was something that could be done but Moore rejected the idea.

After all, he was not unprepared for this. Earlier in the day, they had stolen some concrete blocks and a rope. 'The reason we took these things,' Moore confessed, 'was because I thought I might lose my temper when we saw Olly and I thought I might kill him. I decided if I killed him I would tie him up and put him in the harbour. I got the idea from the Mad Dogs who were going to kill their leader in the same way.'

They drove into the harbour area, coming to a halt between two warehouses.

Moore went on, 'While Al drove him in the van I had been tying him up. I connected the bag to his feet with the bricks in it. We drove straight up to about ten yards from the water in the harbour and turned round and backed up. Al dropped in the bag and I dropped the body. What got Al was the bubbles. What got me was the staring eyes.'

At the trial at Lewes Crown Court, which began on 26th November 1973, Paula Merritt related how Moore had told her on 27th February that he had traced Clive Olive's whereabouts and that he intended to kill him. She had been worried about his obsession with Clive Olive and they had had some arguments over this. She said that he seemed unable to put it out of his mind.

Two days later, when he met her before she went to school, he told her what had happened and that Olly's body was in the harbour. When he confessed to her, Moore had been very jumpy, she said. In the following weeks they had talked about the murder and had agreed that, should the police come to arrest Moore, they would commit suicide. They had talked of jumping off the cliffs at Peacehaven. Speaking of Moore, Paula said she had found him kind, gentle, extremely loving and very protective, and her father agreed with this assessment of Moore.

The court learnt that Olly was 'not a boy of exemplary character' and Paula's father, who had always found Moore well-behaved, said that he shared the young man's sentiments about wanting to teach Olive a lesson for raping his daughter but he had strongly advised him not to take the law into his own hands.

Yet there was another view of Moore which emerged. Defiantly, standing in the dock wearing a bus conductor's jacket and with his red hair tied back in a pony tail, he said that his only regrets were that he was separated from Paula and that he felt no remorse about killing Olive. In fact, he said, 'I think I have done Brighton a favour.' He went on to say, 'I don't feel I have done anything wrong. I knew it was against the law but what he had done was also against the law. He had raped my girl. Nobody else would do it, so I felt it would be my job.'

A psychiatrist, Dr Eric Shepherd, said with regard to Moore, 'After 24 years I am still shockable,' he said. 'I was shocked by this man's callous attitude.' Moore had shown such a cold indifference to what he had done. 'He referred to it as the night he got knocked off. It was a very casual way to talk about somebody who got killed.' Moore hated Olive so much that he refused even to mention his name. He felt justified in his anger and, in Dr Shepherd's view, extremely smug about the offence. He had not, the prosecution would suggest as it followed up the psychiatrist's judgement, tried to see if Olive was alive. Neither he nor the other two had attempted to check the youth's pulse, heart or breathing.

During the course of questioning, Michael Eastham, the prosecution QC, made a reference to Paula and drugs. Moore from the dock called out, 'You shut your mouth or I'll belt you one, mate.' Then, he grabbed a water bottle and threw it at counsel. Not surprisingly, the judge remonstrated with him.

Much was made at the trial of Brian Moore's mental state. One psychiatrist said that he had 'an obsessional, paranoid and somewhat psychotic personality' and that this would impair his actions. His opinion was that it might have been aggravated by taking LSD in the days before he met Paula and that this led to a confusion where reality and fantasy were mixed up. Whilst Moore was sane, he could not form a proper judgment of what he was intending to do to Olive. He might well have been a candidate for treatment.

Moore's counsel, Felix Waley QC, said that Moore had all the cunning of a maniac and killed with the remorseless cruelty of a maniac. He was asking the jury to return a verdict of manslaughter in Moore's case because of diminished responsibility. His client was not mad and not sane but somewhere between the two. He had shown a total lack of concern about Olive's death. When he received the charge sheet, Moore crossed out the name of Olive and wrote the word 'rat'. As an afterthought, he had added, 'and that's an insult to the animal kingdom'.

Albert Dorn's defence counsel, Oliver Martin QC, declared that his client was an 'inadequate and inoffensive person, caught up in the crazy passions of his half-mad brother in law.' Dorn himself said that he had not expected such an outcome but that once the beating started he had been afraid to intervene in case Moore turned on him.

Christine continued to claim that she had played no part in what had occurred in the van. Formerly at an approved school, she was now heavily pregnant, a sad figure with her brother and husband both in a serious plight.

The trial ended on 6th December when, after a jury retirement of nearly seven hours, Moore and Dorn were found guilty of murder and Christine Dorn of manslaughter. The two men were sentenced to life and Christine to ten years. Mr Justice Thesiger referred to the case as 'one of the most horrible murders', adding that he was sure that 'no one minded a bit whether Olive was dead or alive when he was put in the water that night'.

'You bastard,' Christine shouted out as the verdict was announced. In response to this, the Dorns were made life members of the Mad Dogs, a group they had left before the murder. Now their desertion was forgiven. 'Albert and Christine showed great class during the trial,' it was announced. 'It was great when she shouted out "You bastard".'

The next year the men were refused leave to appeal but the conviction against Christine Dorn was reversed. The Court of Appeal declared that she had played no part in the murder or in disposing of the body.

It is a sad case. Most murders are. But here a boy aged 16 suffered an appalling death at the hands of a 21 year old, in the presence of an 18 year old girl and another relatively young man, all four of them captivated by a lifestyle that was squalid and profoundly meaningless. They were all of them prisoners of an empty and violent cult.

(*Paula Merritt is not the real name of the young girl who was involved in this case.*)

BIBLIOGRAPHY

Cawthorne, Nigel *Satanic Murder* Authors on Line 2000
Foot, Paul *Who Framed Colin Wallace?* Macmillan 1995
Gaute, J. H. H. and Odell, Robin *The Murderers' Who's Who*
    Pan Books 1980
Gaute, J. H. H. and Odell, *Murder WhatDunit* Pan Books 1984
Hastings, Macdonald *The Other Mr Churchill* Dodd, Mead
    1965
Herbert, Arthur *All the Sinners* Long 1931
Morton, James *A Calendar Of Killing* Warner Books 1997
Newton, Toyne *The Demonic Connection* Blandford Press 1987
Randles, Jenny and Gough, Peter *Spontaneous Human
    Combustion* Hale 1992
Richardson, Nigel *Breakfast in Brighton* Victor Gollancz 1998
Tullett, Tom *Strictly Murder* The Bodley Head 1979
Wallace, Edgar *The Trial of Patrick Mahon* Scribners 1928
Wilson, Colin *Mammoth Book of True Crime* Robinson 1990

In the preparation of this book I have been heavily dependent on newspaper reports, as many of the cases in which I have been interested have not appeared in book form. May I therefore, without citing each of the many newspapers, acknowledge that I have used nearly every national daily and every newspaper published in East and West Sussex. I have also used the *Picture Post* and several *True Crime* magazines.